THE
MILLWALL
FC
MISCELLANY

DAVID SULLIVAN

FOREWORD BY NEIL HARRIS

First published in 2011 by

The History Press
The Mill, Brimscombe Port
Stroud, Gloucestershire, GL5 2QG
www.thehistorypress.co.uk

British Library Cataloguing in Publication Data.
A catalogue record for this book is available from the British Library.

ISBN 978 0 7524 6077 2

Typesetting and origination by The History Press
Printed in Great Britain

FOREWORD

I am standing in the tunnel ready to take the field, the noise is deafening, the hairs on the back of my neck are standing and I can see my team-mates are filled with nerves, anticipation and probably a sense of fear, feeling the hostility of the atmosphere into which they are about to walk.

The pressure is lifted as we see a Huddersfield team finally emerge from the safety of their dressing room, expressions etched with the fright and dread of having to run the gauntlet of playing at the Den. This recollection from the play-off semi-final in May 2010 epitomises a football club which prides itself on being united between players and supporters.

During the course of this book you will come across numerous episodes of a club that is known worldwide for its motto of 'No One Likes Us, We Don't Care'.

I have been both fortunate and proud to have played a big part in a wonderful club's history, a club that never seems to be more than a game away from its next major incident, whether it's a an FA Cup final, play-off final, promotion, relegation or an FA hearing. This is Millwall.

Neil Harris, 2011

INTRODUCTION

This miscellany is, as far as I am aware, the first of its kind to be published on Millwall. It contains a wealth of facts, trivia, stats, stories and legends. Having celebrated their 125th birthday in 2010, the Lions (since their formation in 1885) have had as many highs as they have had lows. A period of seven years, beginning in 1997, saw the Lions go from administration to the FA Cup final in 2004. To celebrate their 125 years the Lions also finally ended their Wembley hoodoo with victory over Swindon Town in the League One play-off final last year.

On the following pages you will read about the biggest wins and the heaviest defeats, the player who sold his England cap, attendances, and other intriguing curios, like the famous Victorian/Edwardian celebrity who appeared for Millwall, and the singing centre-forward. Along with quotes, unusual statistics and passages from the club's colourful history, this volume is a must for any Lions fan. There are, I am sure, many tales and stories on Millwall that will remain buried until future researchers unearth them, but if you enjoy reading what has already been found then this labour of love will have been worthwhile.

Finally I would like to thank Michelle Tilling at The History Press for her encouragement and the faith she has shown since asking me to compile this book, and for living Lions legend Neil Harris for his foreword. Many publications have been consulted in my research and I would like thank all those authors, known or otherwise, who have assisted me in my quest.

David Sullivan, 2011

THE MISCELLANY

THE BEGINNING

Like many clubs who have survived for over a century or more, Millwall's formation began in very humble circumstances, when in the summer of 1885 a group of workers from a firm of jam and marmalade producers, C. & E. Morton, decided to form a football club. The mix of the group was made up of many Scottish migrant workers and some local lads who decided to jump on the bandwagon, as the game of Association Football was beginning to capture the imagination of young men up and down the country.

The name Millwall evolved from the seven windmills that were originally located along the western wall on the Isle of Dogs. After the name of Millwall Rovers had been agreed, the choice of colours for the playing strip appeared to be a formality. Such was the Caledonian influence in Millwall's formation, the navy blue and white of the flag of St Andrew's cross, the Saltire was adopted.

Who could have imagined that 15 years after being on the end of a 5–0 thumping at the hands of Fillebrook in their first ever match, Millwall Rovers would, as Millwall Athletic, have been prominent in forming and twice winning the Southern League, and reaching their first FA Cup semi-final in 1900. Unfortunately for Millwall, their emerging fame and prominence took a knock in 1897 when their application to join the Football League was rejected. Having received just one vote, this occurrence would delay their appearance to join the elite until 1920, when they became founder members of the new Third Division.

NICKNAMES

Millwall have only ever had two nicknames, the initial one being the Dockers, not surprisingly due their proximity to the Millwall Docks. The second, the Lions as they are known today, could have emanated from two likely sources. One was mentioned following their epic run to their first FA Cup semi-final in 1900 when Millwall were described in the press as the 'lions of the south'. The other was supposedly coined by an enthusiastic fan watching a Millwall match who on many occasions kept shouting out, 'Come on Millwall, eat 'em up!' A nearby chap was getting rather irritated by this 'Eat 'em up' chant and remarked sarcastically, 'Hi what are these fellows, footballers or lions?' The first fan's riposte was, 'Why, lions of course,' who then yelled 'Come on the Lions'. That said, the local press were in the habit of calling them the Blues or the Dark Blues.

BROTHERS

Millwall have fielded a known twelve sets of brothers so far in their history, with the first set of siblings being the Warners of Poplar who appeared in the very early days of the club's existence. George and Henry were fairly regular performers who may have been joined by another brother whose first name began with 'A'. Whoever 'A' was, his contribution was not as prolific as that of his two brothers. George and Arthur Burton were a pair of brothers associated with the club when Millwall Athletic were still an amateur club

Another trio of early stalwarts were Eddie, William and Dick Jones. The Welsh family had settled on the Isle of Dogs with Eddie, aka 'Taff', the first to take the plunge with Millwall Athletic before Willie signed on. Dick, who was English-born, became the third brother to pin his colours to the Millwall mast in 1899. Dick would later become Millwall's third Welsh international in 1906, with two appearances for his country. His association with the club stretched to 1935.

The Caledonian input of siblings began with Henry and James Matthew who spent three and two years respectively with the club, and both gained Southern League championship medals in 1894/95 and 1895/96. Alex Tainsh, who had one season at The Den in 1919/20, had followed his elder brother John down from Scotland – John's spell also lasted for one campaign: 1905/06.

Not only were George and Jack Fisher brothers, they were also twins. As in so many cases, one brother appears to outshine the other, and this was certainly the case with these two. George would go on to play in over 300 games for the club, while Jack would only manage a meagre three starts after signing during the Second World War. A similar tale to the Fishers' was that of the pre-Second World War brothers George and Ken Burditt who played over 63 games between them for Millwall. However, poor old George appeared in just one.

The Emerald Isle would be the next source to supply Millwall, with the Brady brothers from Dublin, Ray and Pat. The two Irishmen (the elder brothers of Liam Brady of Arsenal) had outstanding careers at The Den before both signed for Queens Park Rangers in 1963.

Charlie Hurley was born in Ireland but was brought to England at an early age and signed for Millwall aged 17 in 1953. He would go on to forge a marvellous career with Sunderland after his transfer to them in September 1957. However, his younger brother Chris, despite scoring twice in his first game of the 1964/65 season, would never make the same impact that Charlie had.

Another, more local duo, were Phil and Nick Coleman who came through the youth ranks at Millwall. Phil would later captain the youngsters who won the FA Youth Cup in 1979, but it was Nick who made the most first-team appearances for the Lions. Following on from the Colemans are the Bethnal Green-born John and Brian Sparrow who both had loan moves to The Den. John came in 1977 from Chelsea, while the younger Brian arrived five years later from Arsenal. Meanwhile, North Londoners Dean and John Neal had varied careers at Millwall, with Dean notching 42 goals in 120 league appearances, but John managed just one goal in six matches.

THE BIG HOME DEFEATS

21/2/1948	1–7 v Bury	Division Two
10/10/1960	1–7 v Chelsea	League Cup first round
10/8/2002	0–6 v Rotherham Utd	Division One
11/3/1978	1–6 v Ipswich Town	FA Cup sixth round
5/1/1982	1–6 v Grimsby Town	FA Cup third round
18/9/2010	1–6 v Watford	Championship

THE BIG AWAY DEFEATS

28/1/1946	1–9 v Aston Villa	FA Cup fourth round
16/1/1932	1–8 v Plymouth Argyle	Division Two
22/10/1933	1–7 v Manchester Utd	Division Two
15/12/1956	1–7 v Walsall	Division Three South
25/12/1925	0–6 v Luton Town	Division Three South
3/1/1948	0–6 v Cardiff City	Division Two
17/11/1962	0–6 v Peterborough Utd	Division Three
9/12/1995	0–6 v Sunderland	Division One

KEEP IT ON THE ISLAND

A footballing term that is seldom heard today, 'keep it on the island' is credited to a Millwall giant of the late Victorian era – the strapping full-back Jack Graham – whose famous punts, clearances and passes at the East Ferry Road ground usually exceeded the confines of the pitch. Hence the cries of the supporters of 'keep it on the island!'

CONSECUTIVE CLEAN SHEETS

The most consecutive clean sheets kept by Millwall is 11, when the club were members of Division Three South. The run commenced on 27 February 1926 and was ended with a 3–1 defeat at Exeter City on 17 April. Of the 11 games, the Lions won 9 and drew 2.

Gillingham (H)	0–0
Merthyr Town (A)	2–0
Reading (H)	1–0
Southend United (A)	1–0
Bournemouth (A)	0–0
Brighton & Hove Albion (H)	2–0
QPR (H)	3–0
Watford (H)	3–0
Bristol Rovers (A)	1–0
Watford (A)	1–0
Swindon Town (H)	3–0

SIGNIFICANT UNBEATEN RUNS

The Lions have had two significant unbeaten runs as a Football League club, with the first, at the start of the 1959/60 season, being a 19-match undefeated spell that ended in a 2–1 loss at Notts County (11 of the fixtures finished as draws). The full list with goalscorers is set out below:

22/8/1959	Workington (H)	3–0
		Ackerman, Pierce, Howells
27/8/1959	Doncaster R (A)	0–0
29/8/1959	Rochdale (A)	1–0
		Broadfoot
31/8/1959	Doncaster R (H)	1–1
		Wilson
5/9/1959	Gateshead (H)	4–0
		Crowshaw, Wilson, Ackerman (2)

7/9/1959	Bradford (A)	1–1
		Ackerman
12/9/1959	Darlington (A)	1–1
		Broadfoot
14/9/1959	Bradford (H)	2–0
		Heckman, Howells
19/9/1959	Aldershot (H)	2–0
		Wilson (2)
21/9/1959	Northampton T (A)	3–0
		Broadfoot, Wilson, Ackerman
26/9/1959	Barrow (A)	2–2
		Pierce (2)
28/9/1959	Northampton T (H)	2–1
		Pierce (2)
3/10/1959	Gillingham (H)	3–3
		Broadfoot, Wilson, Crowshaw
5/10/1959	Southport (H)	2–2
		Pierce, Ackerman
10/10/1959	Exeter City(A)	2–2
		Wilson, Broadfoot
17/10/1959	Watford (H)	2–2
		Broadfoot (pen), Wilson
24/10/1959	Oldham Ath (A)	1–1
		Howells
28/10/1959	Crystal Palace (A)	2–1
		Broadfoot, Wilson
31/10/1959	Carlisle Utd (A)	1–1
		Pierce

The second such exploit was the magnificent 59-game unbeaten at home from 24 August 1964 until 14 January 1967. Coincidentally, the run began and ended against clubs from Devon; Torquay United who drew 2–2 and then Plymouth Argyle who ended the run with a 2–1 success. The details are set out below.

24/8/1964	Torquay Utd	2–2
		Curran, Whitehouse
29/8/1964	York City	1–1
		Curran
7/9/1964	Chester	1–0
		Opponent own goal

12/9/1964	Brighton & Hove A	2–0 D.A.B. Jones, Whitehouse
26/9/1964	Barrow	3–1 K. Jones, Hurley (2)
28/9/1964	Southport	0–0
10/10/1964	Tranmere R	1–0 Curran
12/10/1964	Bradford City	3–0 D.A.B. Jones, Curran, Rowan
24/10/1964	Crewe Alex	0–0
7/11/1964	Halifax T	5–1 Julians (3), Rowan, Neil
21/11/1964	Chesterfield	4–2 Whitehouse, Julians (2), John
12/12/1964	Stockport C	1–0 Whitehouse
26/12/1964	Wrexham	2–2 Wilson, John
2/1/1965	Lincoln City	2–1 Curran, Julians
23/1/1965	Oxford Utd	2–2 Curran (2, both pens)
13/2/1965	Hartlepool Utd	0–0
27/2/1965	Darlington	1–1 Clarke
13/3/1965	Newport C	4–0 Curran, K. Jones (2), Brown
27/3/1965	Notts County	4–1 John (pen), Rowan (2), Julians
5/4/1965	Aldershot	5–0 Julians (2), Curran (2), Clarke
10/4/1965	Doncaster R	1–1 Clarke
16/4/1965	Rochdale	0–0
24/4/1965	Bradford	1–0 Gilchrist
21/8/1965	Workington	2–0 Curran, Clarke

4/9/1965	Oldham Ath	1–0
		Julians
13/9/1965	Exeter City	3–0
		Jones, Rowan, Neil
18/9/1965	Scunthorpe Utd	2–2
		Jacks, Julians
2/10/1965	QPR	2–1
		Julians (2)
16/10/1965	Swindon T	1–0
		Brown
25/10/1965	Bristol R	3–3
		Opponent own goal, Julians, Brown
30/10/1965	Grimsby T	2–1
		Julians, Wilson
22/11/1965	Peterborough	4–1
		McQuade, Brown, Julians (2)
27/11/1965	Oxford Utd	2–0
		Julians, Brown
11/12/1965	Walsall	1–1
		Curran
28/12/1965	Hull City	3–0
		Julians, Curran, Neil
1/1/1966	Southend Utd	2–0
		Neil, Cripps
15/1/1966	Shrewsbury T	4–2
		Wilson, Julians, Brown, Rowan
5/2/1966	Gillingham	2–0
		Julians (2)
26/2/1966	Watford	0–0
5/3/1966	Reading	3–0
		Wilson, Julians, Cripps (pen)
19/3/1966	Brighton	3–2
	& Hove A	Julians, Dunphy, Jacks
2/4/1966	Brentford	1–0
		Brown
12/4/1966	Bournemouth	1–0
		Julians
16/4/1966	York City	2–0
		Dunphy, Wilson

30/4/1966	Swansea Town	1–0	
		Jones	
16/5/1966	Mansfield Town	2–0	
		Opponent own goal, Brown	
27/8/1966	Charlton Ath	0–0	
3/9/1966	Northampton T	1–0	
		Julians	
5/9/1966	Coventry City	1–0	
		Broadfoot	
17/9/1966	Hull City	2–1	
		Wilson, Julians	
19/9/1966	Preston North End	2–0	
		Opponent own goal, Neil	
1/10/1966	Birmingham City	3–1	
		Julians, Neil, Broadfoot	
15/10/1966	Crystal Palace	1–1	
		Hunt	
29/10/1966	Cardiff City	1–0	
		Baker	
12/11/1966	Ipswich Town	1–0	
		Hunt	
26/11/1966	Carlisle United	2–1	
		Julians (2)	
10/12/1966	Bolton Wanderers	2–0	
		Julians, Neil	
17/12/1966	Rotherham United	2–0	
		Hunt, Wilson (pen)	
26/12//1966	Norwich City	2–1	
		Julians (2)	

Pld	W	D	L	F	A
59	43	16	0	112	33

MOST AWAY WINS IN A SEASON

The most impressive campaign for victories away from home has to be the 2008/09 season when Millwall won 12 league games and two FA Cup ties.

13/9/2008	Leicester City	1–0
		Alexander
28/9/2008	Swindon T	2–1
		Easter, Grabban
11/10/2008	Tranmere R	3–1
		Kandol (2), Abdou
21/10/2008	Colchester Utd	2–1
		Grabban, Robinson
13/12/2008	Walsall	2–1
		Harris, Frampton
27/1/2009	Hereford Utd	2–0
		Craig, Laird
24/2/2009	Cheltenham T	3–1
		Henry (pen), Grimes, Laird
3/3/2009	Southend Utd	1–0
		Alexander
7/3/2009	Huddersfield T	2–1
		Laird, Henry
17/3/2009	MK Dons	1–0
		Laird
21/3/2009	Hartlepool Utd	3–2
		Harris (3)
28/3/2009	Crewe Alex	1–0
		Price

The two FA Cup victories came at Chester City (3–0) and in a third round replay at Crewe (3–2).

NOW THAT'S LONGEVITY

When Millwall faced Crystal Palace at Cold Blow Lane in October 1966, there was one interested spectator in the shape of 82-year-old William (Bill) Gaffney. It was reported that Bill had attended Millwall Athletic's first match as a professional concern in 1894 and was also present at the Lions' initial game against Brighton & Hove Albion at The Den in October 1910.

GROUNDS

Millwall have played home games on six different grounds since their formation.

1885–6	Glengall Road
1886–90	Lord Nelson
1890–1901	East Ferry Road
1901–10	North Greenwich
1910–93	The Den, Cold Blow Lane
1993–	New Den, Zampa Road

NB: Millwall have, owing to ground closures, played homes games at Selhurst Park (December 1947) and Fratton Park (April 1978).

BIG HOME VICTORIES

29 August 1927
9–1 v Torquay United, Division Three South
scorers: Hawkins (3), Landells, Phillips (2), Bryant (3)

19 November 1927
9–1 v Coventry City, Division Three South
scorers: Landells (4), Cock (2), Phillips (2), Collins

19 September 1925
8–1 v Southend United, Division Three South
scorers: Dillimore (3), Graham, Moule, Parker (2), Chance

19 December 1925
7–0 v Luton Town, Division Three South
scorers: Landells (2), Amos (2, both pens), Gore, Moule, Dillimore

27 December 1926
7–0 v Luton Town, Division Three South
scorers: Amos, Phillips (2), Gomm (2), Parker (2)

12 December 1936
7–0 v Gateshead, FA Cup second round
scorers: Mangnall, Thorogood, McCartney, K. Burditt (3),
Thomas (pen)

30 October 1937
7–0 v Torquay United, Division Three South
scorers: Steele, Mangnall (3), Walsh (2), Brolly

BIG AWAY VICTORIES

7 May 1927
6–1 v Crystal Palace, Division Three South
scorers: Parker (3, 1 a pen), Black, Phillips, Bryant

24 December 1927
6–1 v Bristol Rovers, Division Three South
scorers: Cock (2), Black, Phillips (2), own goal

28 November 1936
6–1 Aldershot FA Cup first round
scorers: Thorogood, Mangnall (4, 1 a pen), Thomas

17 September 1938
6–1 v Manchester City, Division Two
scorers: Barker (2), Walsh, Rawlings (2), Richardson

11 January 1938
5–0 v York City, FA Cup third round
scorers: McLeod (4), Rawlings

6 February 1965
5–0 v Barrow, Division Four
scorers: Julians, Curran, Rowan, Whitehouse (2)

CHARLIE'S FLIGHT OF FANCY

During the course of the Berlin Airlift of 1948–9, Lions manager Charlie Hewitt cottoned on to the idea of flying in two continental players every week to play for Millwall at the approximate cost of £1,000, citing the success of the mercy flights to the German capital and how it easy it would be to pull-off such a coup. Needless to say, Hewitt's flight never 'took-off'.

INTERNATIONAL VENUE

The Dens (both old and new) have staged international matches (men's), with the first being a home international between England and Wales on 13 March 1911, which England won 3–0 in front of a gate of 25,000. Then, on 12 December 1989, a 'B' fixture between England and Yugoslavia was staged, again the English coming out on top with a 2–1 success. To celebrate the construction of the New Den in 1993, Poland were the visitors for a UEFA under-21 European Championship encounter on 7 September. Unfortunately, England could not maintain their winning run at Millwall as the Poles edged a 2–1 win.

On 21 August 2007 the club hosted a friendly international between Ghana and Senegal that finished in a 1–1 draw. Two other national teams to feature at New Den were Jamaica and Nigeria, who shared a goalless draw on 11 February 2009.

JIMMY BROAD

In the three games Jim was absent in Millwall's last season of Southern League football in 1919/20, the Lions failed to score. The reliance on Jim was all too evident when he notched 32 goals in 39 appearances. His tally is all the more remarkable when you consider that he did not find the net in 15 of the games he played in. Joint second goalscorers in that campaign were Dougie Thomson and Bobby Noble, who both scored 4.

FA YOUTH CUP

Millwall have won the FA Youth Cup on two occasions, with the first arriving in 1978/79. The first team had been relegated that year, so it was left to the juniors to lift the gloom pervading The Den. Twelve years later came the second success.

1978/79

R2	Slough Town	3–0
R3	Norwich City	2–0
R4	Sunderland	2–1
R5	Nottingham Forest	3–3
R5 (replay)	Nottingham Forest	1–0
SF first leg	Everton	0–0
SF second leg	Everton	2–0
F first leg	Manchester City	0–0
F second leg	Manchester City	2–0

1990/91

R1	Sutton United	5–0
R2	Swindon Town	1–0
R3	Portsmouth	3–1
R4	Plymouth Argyle	1–0
R5	Wimbledon	1–1
R5 (replay)	Wimbledon	3–2
SF first leg	West Ham Utd	2–1
SF second leg	West Ham Utd	2–0
F first leg	Sheffield Wednesday	3–0
F second leg	Sheffield Wednesday	0–0

CRICKETING LIONS

Many professional footballers could turn their hand to the summer game of cricket, though the days of combining both sports have long since gone. The last Lion to be classed as such was goalkeeper Jim Standen who regularly appeared for Worcestershire. Former England bowler and outside-left Dave Smith played for Gloucestershire, while Millwall reserve full-back Terry Kent assisted Essex as did 1920s Millwall players Len Graham and Alf Moule.

South African Test cricketer Lennox Brown played one game for Millwall against Crystal Palace in 1935. Two years earlier, Laurie Fishlock, the England and Surrey player, appeared in 34 games for Millwall at outside-left and would finish up as leading goalscorer with 7.

Then there were two players from the Southern League days, Willie Stewart and David Storrier, who both played for Forfarshire in their native Scotland as well as making appearances for the Lions. When Millwall were still an amateur outfit, another of their cricketing players was Charlie McGahey who played for Essex and, later, England.

SUBSTITUTES

With substitutes being allowed since 1965, the bench size has gradually increased so that now clubs are permitted to name seven players for that role, with three allowed to replace a colleague at any point of the game's duration. Millwall's first sub was George Jacks who replaced Kenny Jones to a chorus of boos in the very first match of the 1965/66 season against Workington at The Den – the Lions won 2–0.

The first player to score a hat-trick after coming on as a substitute was the American striker John Kerr who achieved the feat against Derby County in August 1994. Besides this, John has the unique

New Den distinction of scoring both the first goal in the new stadium, in the official opening match against Sporting Lisbon, and the first League goal, versus Southend United.

. Neil Harris, the Lions' record goalscorer, became the second Millwall player to register a hat-trick as a substitute, when he bagged a 9-minute treble to overturn a 2-goal deficit into a winning margin of 3–2 at Hartlepool United on 21 March 2009.

MOST APPEARANCES

Listed below are the top ten appearance makers for Millwall in all competitions:

Barry Kitchener	602	1966–82
Keith Stevens	557	1980–99
Harry Cripps	445	1961–75
Neil Harris	430	1997–2005 & 2006–11
Alan McLeary	413	1982–93 & 1996–9
Dick Hill	393	1919–30
John Joyce	385	1900–2 & 1903–10
Len Graham	363	1923–34
Jimmy Forsyth	350	1929–39
Bryan King	340	1967–76

MOST GOALS

The all-important top ten in the list of leading goalscorers for the Lions in all competitions is as follows:

Neil Harris	138	Alf Twigg	88
Teddy Sheringham	111	Derek Possee	87
John Calvey	98	Jimmy Constantine	83
Jack Cock	92	Johnny Shepherd	82
Wally Davis	91	John Landells	77

LUCKY SEVEN

Over 50 years have elapsed since Millwall dismantled Chester 7–1 in a Fourth Division fixture at The Den back in April 1960. How many of the 9,647 fans in attendance would have realised that Millwall would be still waiting to hit another seven over half a century later?

However, if you count the friendly match against Dundee in August 1968, which Millwall won 8–0, then you have to regard this as their biggest victory. The amazing thing to come out of the Chester game was that, with around 22 minutes to go, Millwall were only leading by one goal. However, when a disputed penalty was awarded and converted, the floodgates opened to devastating effect.

For the record the marksmen for the Lions were Barry Pierce with two, Pat Brady, the scorer of the penalty, and further goals were added by Alf Ackerman, Dave Smith and Dave Harper. Chester centre-half Bill Spruce also assisted with an own goal.

NATIONAL VISITORS

A Canadian XI, in their thirty-sixth match of a marathon six-month tour of the UK, was the first overseas team to play Millwall Athletic. The game, which was played at East Ferry Road on 21 November 1891, was witnessed by a crowd of about 2,000 spectators, and ended in a 1–1 draw. However, the Dockers had to wait until the last ten minutes for their goal when Peter Banks was on hand to equalise from Frank McCulloch's fine centre.

After Millwall had turned professional the first representative team to visit them was a German select team. Their fact-finding tour in 1896, four years before the formation of the DFB (the German FA), found them on the receiving end of many heavy defeats but Millwall's winning margin of 9–0 was their biggest loss. John Calvey led the rout with four goals, Alex McKenzie scored a brace while Arthur Millar, Joe Davies and Alf Geddes got one each.

In their preparation for the 1968 Olympic Games, the Italian Olympic XI visited The Den in August 1967 for a warm-up fixture and were defeated by the only goal, when Keith Weller scored direct from a corner. Another national team to visit was the United Arab Emirates who Millwall defeated 3–1 on 21 August 1984. However, this match was played at Harlow.

Millwall were due to face the national team of Iran in July 2005 but, following the London bombing outrage earlier in the month, the fixture had to be cancelled amid security fears.

The Unity in the Community Cup was first contested (and for the only time so far) in 2007 when Millwall entertained the national team of Sierra Leone. The Lions recorded a 2–1 win with goals from Neil Harris after four minutes and Gary Alexander's late strike in the ninetieth minute after Kargbo had drawn the Africans level in the sixteenth minute. The teams that day were:

Millwall: Day (Edwards), Senda (Barron), Robinson (Whitbread), Shaw, Frampton, Spiller (Fuseini), Brammer (Hackett), Dunne (Smith), Harris, Alexander, May (Ardley)

Sierra Leone: Caulker, Jalloh (Ngongu), Deen, Sama, Kallou, Kanu, Conteh, Kadi (M. Kamara), Din-Sesay (Dumbuya), Bah, Kargbo (R. Kamara)

KENT FA CHALLENGE CUP FINALS

This was an annual fixture normally played towards the end of the season with the inaugural game taking place in April 1946 when Millwall faced Gillingham at their Priestfield Stadium. These two teams contested the first two finals, before Millwall took on Charlton Athletic for the next few years, although Gillingham did reappear again in 1952. However, following Charlton's win in 1967 the fixture went into hibernation. That was until 1975 when it made its comeback as pre-season tournament that involved the three clubs already mentioned here, as well as Crystal

Palace. Following the 1976/77 season, Millwall and Gillingham faced Brentford and Aldershot. However, due to lack of interest the trophy was mothballed. Listed here are finals the Lions have participated in.

1945/46	Gillingham	2–2	Millwall (aet)
1947/48	Millwall	4–0	Gillingham 0
1948/49	Charlton Athletic	1–1	Millwall (aet)
1949/50	Millwall	0–0	Charlton Athletic
Replay	Charlton Athletic	2–1	Millwall
1950/51	Millwall	6–1	Charlton Athletic
1951/52	Millwall	1–0	Gillingham
1952/53	Millwall	3–2	Charlton Athletic
1953/54	Millwall	2–3	Charlton Athletic
1954/55	Millwall	2–4	Charlton Athletic
1955/56	Millwall	3–3	Charlton Athletic
1956/57	Millwall	3–0	Charlton Athletic
1957/58	Millwall	1–2	Charlton Athletic
1958/59	Millwall	1–1	Charlton Athletic (aet)
1959/60	Millwall	1–2	Charlton Athletic
1960/61	Millwall	1–5	Charlton Athletic
1961/62	Millwall	3–0	Charlton Athletic
1963/64	Millwall	1–1	Charlton Athletic
1964/65	Millwall	0–5	Charlton Athletic
1966/67	Charlton Athletic	3–2	Millwall

Victories: Millwall 6, Charlton Athletic 8

FESTIVAL OF BRITAIN

In May 1951 the country's football fans were treated to a feast of football. The Festival of Britain was held to commemorate the centenary of the Great Exhibition of 1851 and part of the festivities comprised a series of friendly matches. The Lions hosted three games. Firstly they played against the Dutch team HFC Haarlem which finished in a 3–3 draw in front of 9,060 fans. An excellent crowd of 16,204 saw two goals from Johnny Short beat Dundee United 2–1. The final game, against the Belgian club RSC Anderlecht, was a contentious (and a tad nasty) affair that Millwall won 2–1, Jimmy Constantine and a Frank Neary penalty contributing the goals.

THE YOUNG ONES

Millwall have been fortunate in not to having to rely on blooding players of tender years, but one who was highly rated was Moses Ashikodi who came on as a substitute at Brighton in February 2003. The top eight Lion cubs to make their Millwall debuts are as follows:

Moses Ashikodi 15 years 240 days
   v Brighton & Hove Albion, February 2003

David Mehmet   16 years 163 days
   v Burnley, May 1977

Vic Rouse   16 years 227days
   v Chelsea (London Challenge Cup), October 1952

John Richardson   16 years 255 days
   v Middlesbrough (League Cup third round replay), October 1965

David Martin   16 years 335 days
   v Rotherham United, April 1980

Roy Summersby 17 years 31 days
   v Exeter City, April 1952

Curtis Weston   17 years 106 days
   v Bradford City, May 2004

Albert Pritchard 17 years 153 days
   v Bristol City (Third Division South Cup), March 1938

GOLDEN GOAL

Millwall's only game in which the 'Golden Goal' rule applied came at New Den in February 1999 when Richard Sadlier netted the all-important goal in the ninety-seventh minute in an excellent Auto Windscreen 25 contest against Gillingham.

CHRISTMAS DAY

Millwall played their final Christmas Day match at home to Chester in 1958, where the visitors won by the solitary goal. Their record on Christmas Day in the Football League is:

Pld 39   W 15   D 11   L 13   F 52   A 55

While their record during Southern League days shows a similar balance:

Pld 16   W 7   D 3   L 6   F 20   A 20

THE INTERNATIONAL BRIGADE

Free movement within the European Union has seen clubs like Millwall employ the services of not only EU-born players over the last twenty years, but also footballers from all around the world, who have also filtered down into the lower reaches of English football. The Lions have, in all, used players from 29 different countries, besides those from the home countries and the Republic of Ireland. These below were born outside the United Kingdom who have appeared in the first team.

Australia – Lucas Neill, Tim Cahill, Jason van Blerk,
  Alistair Edwards, Carl Veart, David Oldfield
Belgium – Christophe Kinet, Bob Peeters, Pat van den Hauwe,
  W.I. Bryant
Holland – Berry Powel
France – Nadjim Abdou, Sammy Mawene,
  Zoumana Bakayogo, Abou Fofana, Hameur Bouazza
South Africa – Lennox Brown, Alf Ackerman,
  Derek Smethurst
Canada – Josh Simpson, Adrian Serioux, John Kerr
USA – Kasey Keller, Bruce Murray, Junior McDougald,
  Zak Whitbread
Germany – Wilf Smith, Uwe Fuchs
Portugal – Filipe Morais, Carlos Fangueiro
Denmark – Poul Hübertz, Jens Berthel Askou
Russia – Vasili Kulkov
Ukraine – Sergei Yuran, Sergei Baltacha
Ghana – Kim Grant, Ali Fuseini
Surinam – Etienne Verveer, Romano Sion
Trinidad & Tobago – John Granville
Jamaica – Trevor Robinson
Uganda – Andrew Iga
Nigeria – Moses Ashikodi, Danny Shittu
Venezuela – Giovanni Savarese
Egypt – Hussein Hegazi
Cyprus – Danis Salman
Brazil – Juan Maldonado
Malawi – Tamika Mkandawire
Barbados – Alf Kingsley
Croatia – Ahmet Brkovic
Guadeloupe – Willy Gueret
Democratic Republic of Congo – Tresor Kandol
Cameroon – Vincent Pericard
Norway – Jo Tessem

THE FIRST GOALSCORING SUBSTITUTE

Ronnie 'Butch' Howell became the first Millwall substitute to score in a match – against Middlesbrough at The Den in an FA Cup third round replay in January 1969 (his FA Cup debut). Butch's first meaningful touch in the sixty-sixth minute resulted in the game's only goal after he replaced Billy Neil. It was also Howell's first game of the season, and his first and only goal for the Lions. A second youngster to score on his FA Cup debut as a substitute was Dave Mehmet who achieved his feat against Ipswich Town in March 1978.

RED CARD DEBUT

Having a player sent off is galling at the best of times, but spare a thought for the participant who gets his marching orders on his debut. Listed below are those known Lions who suffered this embarrassment:

Alan Noble
    v Brighton & Hove Albion   10 September 1927

Carl Emberson
    v Crystal Palace   14 September 1993

Stephen McPhail
    v Sheffield Wednesday   16 February 2002

Jermaine Easter
    v Swindon Town   28 September 2008

Darren Carter
    v Bristol City   7 August 2010

Jens Berthel Askou
    v Leicester City   22 January 2011

HA' WAY THE LADS

Three strikers from the north-east have scored over 30 goals in a season for Millwall, with Dick Parker from Stockton-on-Tees hitting what looks like an unbeatable 37 league goals in 1926/27. Dick's total was nearly reached the following campaign when John Landells (of Gateshead stock) managed 33 goals. However, Jack Calvey from South Bank, Middlesbrough, managed to bang in 33 goals on two occasions in 1896/97 and 1898/99, although Jack's tallies were obtained in all competitions.

ODE TO BARRY KITCHENER

There have been many odes and verses written about Millwall's derring-do, and this excellent one, penned by long-time fan Bob McCree, was published in 1975 for Barry Kitchener's testimonial.

In honour of the Mighty Kitch
Tonight we gather to honour the 'Mighty Kitch'
No greater Lion supreme as ever strode our famous pitch.
Without a stopper in sixty-seven, the Lions were in a twitch.
'Twas then we first saw the young giant called Kitch.
So True, So Loyal, blimey Barry you're almost Royal.

Through season after season and consecutive game after game
There arose the steadfast Barry who really made his name.
On the ground, in the air, with resolution, but gentle
He always gets his way, but is never, never temperamental.
Amiable, capable, blimey Barry you've been reliable.

We really do appreciate the part he has played,
A fine and true example of how great Lions are made.
He always plays without anger, bitterness or affray,
A fine and true example of showing us all the right way.
So tall, commanding and magnifique, blimey Barry you've
  been fantistique.

And so tonight after great service, we are here for
 Barry's testimonial,
Against Spurs it will be a great night, right ceremonial.
For many, many years we all wish Barry to keep his old job,
 And so this very special night the most deserving chance to make,
 'a nice few bob'.

NON-LEAGUE XI

This would be a decent team for Millwall to field in the Football
League comprising some of the players that have been recruited
from non-league football since the Second World War.

1. Alex Stepney (Tooting & Mitcham United) or Bryan King
    (Chelmsford City)
2. Kenny Cunningham (Tolka Rovers, Dublin)
3. Pat Brady (Home Farm, Dublin)
4. Dave Bumstead (Tooting & Mitcham United)
5. Neil Emblen (Sittingbourne)
6. Hugh Curran (Corby Town)
7. Barry Rowan (Dover)
8. Scott Taylor (Staines Town)
9. Neil Harris (Cambridge City)
10. Steve Morison (Stevenage Borough)
11. Phil Walker (Epsom & Ewell)

THE FLYING DUTCHMAN

Not many Millwall fans would have heard of Gerrit Keizer, a
young Dutch goalkeeper who signed for the Lions as an amateur in
December 1929, at the age of 19. He had originally joined Ajax of
Amsterdam as a 16-year-old. However, he never made a first team
appearance at The Den, but subsequently played for both Arsenal
and Charlton Athletic where he played in 12 and 17 league games
respectively.

Typically eccentric, as goalkeepers go, he failed to keep a clean sheet for the Gunners, before joining Queens Park Rangers. Retuning to Ajax in 1933 he was later to win two caps with the Dutch national side in 1934. Surviving the Second World War he was imprisoned for six months for smuggling British currency in 1947, but following his release he went on to become one of Amsterdam's prominent greengrocers. Gerrit, or 'Gerry' as he was known, earned his sobriquet for playing for the Arsenal on the Saturday before flying home to appear for Ajax on the Sunday.

QUICKEST GOALS

Millwall have scored some very quick goals (in less than a minute) over the years and listed below are those that have been recorded.

Date	Scorer	Oppt	Res	Time (seconds)
2/1/1971	Derek Possee	Charlton Athletic	2–0	8
25/9/1963	John McLaughlin	Newport County	4–3	15
16/8/2008	Trésor Kandol	Oldham Athletic	3–4	15
7/2/1970	Keith Weller	Blackpool	1–1	18
20/10/2000	Neil Harris	Stoke City	2–3	15/19*
14/12/2002	Steve Claridge	Leicester City	1–4	19
11/9/1960	Joe Broadfoot	Oldham Athletic	3–2	30
18/11/1972	Gordon Bolland	QPR	3–1	30
14/4/1999	Kim Grant	Colchester United	2–0	34
28/3/1993	Jamie Moralee	West Ham United	2–2	35

4/11/1978	Opponent own goal	Oldham Athletic	2–3	40
9/9/1989	Teddy Sheringham	Coventry City	4–1	44
19/11/2000	Neil Harris	Leigh RMI	3–0	44**
10/9/1988	Teddy Sheringham	Charlton Athletic	3–0	45
8/9/1982	Willie Carr	Bournemouth	2–0	50
2/1/1971	Derek Possee	Stoke City	1–2	55
21/8/1976	Terry Shanahan	Notts County	2–1	58

* It depends on what newspaper you read.
** A penalty was awarded after 12 seconds.

PENALTY SHOOT-OUTS

Millwall have been involved in 13 penalty shoot-outs, winning 5 and losing 8 (including the last 5). These scenarios have come against different opposition on each occasion and have covered five different competitions. Millwall's victory over Chelsea in 1995 is the pick of the successes when American goalkeeper Kasey Keller became the hero when he saved John Spencer's effort.

In the Lions' first ever shoot-out, with Colchester United in 1976, an amazing ten goals were scored in three games, which still failed to find a winner, and after 300 minutes plus penalties it was Millwall who prevailed. However, the 1997 shoot-out with Northampton Town in the League Cup descended into a farce, after John Gayle had equalised in the last minute to level the aggregate score.

Missing three of their spot-kicks, Millwall scraped home when Kim Grant and Kenny Brown saw them through 2–0. However, Northampton missed four of their allowance with goalkeeper Tim Carter saving three of them, in front of a disbelieving crowd.

The full list is as follows:

September 1976
  v Colchester United (A) League Cup   Won 4–2

October 1985
  v Southampton (A) Milk Cup   Lost 4–5

November 1988
  v Barnsley (H) Full Members' Cup   Won 3–0

December 1990
  v Norwich City (A) Full Members' Cup   Lost 5–6

October 1992
  v Arsenal (H) Rumbelows League Cup   Lost 1–3

January 1995
  v Chelsea (A) FA Cup fourth round   Won 5–4

August 1997
  v Northampton Town (H) Coca-Cola Cup   Won 2–0

February 1999
  v AFC Bournemouth (A) Auto Windscreens   Won 4–3
                            Shield

January 2001
  v Swindon Town (H) Auto Windscreens   Lost 2–3
                            Shield

September 2002
  v Rushden & Diamonds (A) Worthington Cup   Lost 3–5

November 2005
  v Birmingham City (H) Carling Cup   Lost 3–4

November 2006
  v Brighton & Hove Albion (H) Football   Lost 2–3
                            League Trophy

January 2010
  v Derby County (A) FA Cup third round replay Lost 3–5

THE SAD TALE OF JOHN 'JACK' CALVEY

One of Millwall's most prolific goalscorers from their Southern League days was Jack Calvey, who had been recommended to Millwall Athletic by another giant of the club, J.H. (Joe) Gettins, the famous Corinthians player, in February 1896. On seeing his new team-mates play for the first time, Jack was filled with apprehension as to his ability to hold his own in such company. His fears proved to be unfounded when, in an explosive start to his career, he scored a hat-trick on his debut in the 8–1 thrashing of Ilford. Jack would finish the season with 6 goals from 5 matches. Over the course of the next three campaigns he would regularly plunder goals at will with many arriving via his speciality ground shot into the corner of the net.

Despite the regularity of finding the target and for all his efforts down at the East Ferry Road, the only honour bestowed upon him for all this output was a United League title in 1897, a competition in which he nearly scored a goal a game. So, after three full seasons on the Isle of Dogs, John moved to pastures new, signing for Nottingham Forest in May 1899. The story goes that Jack had pitched himself in an East Midlands hotel to offer his talent to the highest bidder, and if true, it was Forest who prevailed.

It was said that Jack's time at the City Ground was disappointing, but his record there bears up to scrutiny and he must have done something right for he was awarded his one England cap against Ireland in Belfast in March 1902. After serving Forest for five years he returned to Millwall, then aged 28, in 1904. The 1904/05 season was to be his last with the Lions and he duly signed for the newly formed Chelsea club in 1905. However, he never appeared in the Pensioners' first team and was eventually forced into retirement with a troublesome knee injury.

There began a new phase in his life when, residing in Poplar and with a family to support, he became a stevedore. The deprivation in the 1920s affected millions and it was no different for Jack. These circumstances may have forced him to part with his sole England cap, no doubt for a pittance as it was purchased by a customer in the Magnet and Dewdrop public house on the West Ferry Road (a later landlord of this watering hole was the former Millwall player Brian Brown, who became the guv'nor in 1976). When Jack died in January 1937, hardly remembered other than by his immediate family and close friends, it seemed to underline the downturn in his life when he was borne to St Patrick's Cemetery, Leytonstone, where he was interred in a pauper's grave.

THE MATCH THAT TOOK 126 DAYS TO COMPLETE

When Millwall were leading Thames Ironworks by two goals to nil in a Southern League fixture at Canning Town on 23 December 1899, the referee abandoned the game after 69 minutes due to the worsening fog that was descending over the Memorial Ground. With no new date arranged, a solution was settled upon to play the remaining minutes following the last scheduled fixture of the season between the two teams at the East Ferry Road on 28 April 1900.

A short break followed the full 90 minute exertions (which West Ham had won 1–0). Then the outstanding 21 minutes were played out with no further goals added to the ones scored by Willy Dryburgh and John Brearley back in December. The game was finally completed with the result standing at 2–0. This, despite Millwall having five changes to the original line-up. The players involved from the first game and the five players who played in the remainder are listed here for posterity: Dave Clear (Walter Cox), Charlie Burgess, Bill 'Wiggy' Davis (Ned Allan), John Fitzpatrick (Dave Smith), Hugh Goldie, Arthur Millar, Willy Dryburgh, John Brearley, Hugh Robertson (Sandy Caie), Bert Banks and Nicol (J.H. 'Joe' Gettins).

FIRST INTERNATIONAL CAP

The honour to become Millwall's first international went not to an Englishman or a Scot, but to Welshman Joe Davies whose only cap while at Millwall came against England in 1897 at Bramall Lane, the home ground of one of Joe's previous clubs, Sheffield United. It was not a happy return for Joe as the Welsh went down 4–0. During his time at United, Joe was suspended for two weeks by the Blades directors for having his 'digs' in a local public house.

THE DAY WAR BROKE OUT

Great Britain's declaration of war against Germany on 3 September 1939 saw the immediate suspension of competitive football, after just three matches. This meant that all the opening fixtures for the 1939/40 season were expunged from the records, including this trio of Millwall's games in Division Two.

Date	Result
26 August 1939	Millwall 3–0 Newcastle United
28 August 1939	Millwall 0–2 Plymouth Argyle
2 September 1939	Bradford Park Avenue 2–2 Millwall

This action deprived Millwall's close-season signing from Portsmouth, Jim Beattie, of his only league appearances for the Lions and the centre-forward's only goal for the club was scored on the last Saturday before the declaration.

When the Football League programme resumed following hostilities the original fixture list for the 1939/40 season was resurrected and restarted, and Millwall found themselves a point worse off after three games.

Date	Result
31 August 1946	Millwall 1–4 Newcastle United
2 September 1946	Millwall 1–1 Plymouth Argyle
7 September 1946	Bradford Park Avenue 0–0 Millwall

Irish international wing-half Tom Brolly was the only Millwall player to appear in all six matches, while outside-left Harry Osman played in five. The only other members of those pre-war teams to resume their careers at The Den in 1946 besides Brolly and Osman were Walter McMillen and George Williams.

THE SHAKESPEARIAN ACTOR WHO PLAYED FOR MILLWALL

A most unusual name in the list of Millwall players is that of George Robey, the famous comedian and star who appeared in three Western League fixtures for the Lions. Two came in the momentous season of 1902/03, in encounters against Reading and Brentford, both of which Millwall won. His last match came against Spurs in April 1907 and ended goalless. In Robey's three appearances, Millwall kept three clean sheets and all the matches were played at North Greenwich.

George Robey (real name George Edward Wade) was born at Herne Hill on 20 September 1864, had a very middle-class upbringing and was educated in both England and Germany. He had been destined for the University of Leipzig and then Cambridge on his return home, but an academic role appeared not to be for George and it was a chance visit to a theatre that led him to a career treading the boards.

He volunteered to be hypnotised and so well did he perform that he became an unpaid assistant. Indeed, while he was under hypnosis, George's singing earned him a professional engagement by the manager of Royal Aquarium in Victoria. Robey was a great friend of football and on many occasions organised charity games for various causes. He became known as the 'Prime Minister of

Mirth' during his performances in the Victorian and Edwardian music halls, and was one of the great pantomime dames.

As his career advanced he took on more serious roles, playing Falstaff in Shakespeare's *Henry V* on stage in 1935, and a dying Falstaff in Laurence Olivier's film version of the same play. He had appeared in silent films such as *Don Quixote* in 1923 but it was as a singer that he commenced his wonderful career, and the song most associated with him was 'If You Were the Only Girl in the World'. He was undoubtedly a man of many talents and for the services he rendered to the country he was knighted in 1954. Not long afterwards George Robey passed away at Saltdean, Sussex, on 29 November 1954, aged 85.

MOST HOME GOALS

Millwall recorded the most home goals in the record-breaking 1927/28 campaign with 87 out of 127 total goals scored, a record for Division Three South. That works out to just a tad over 4 goals per game in a 21-match home programme. The entertaining net-busters were: Landells 25, Phillips 22, Cock 17, Bryant 8, Hawkins 5, Black 3, Chance 2 and Amos 2, while Collins, Page and Parker each netted 1 apiece.

THE MAN IN THE HOT-SEAT

Other than the honorary team managers like Fred Kidd, Edward Stopher and George Saunders, Millwall have had 30 other incumbents of the managerial hot-seat, with Charlie Hewitt also doubling up as secretary. Hewitt is one of three men to have held the position twice, with Ron Gray and John Docherty being the others. As players, 14 of this select band have played international football and the full list overleaf shows which country they appeared for and how many caps they each won.

Name	Time at Millwall	Country	Caps
Bert Lipsham	1911–18	England	1
Bob Hunter	1918–33		
Billy McCracken	1933–6	Ireland	16
Charlie Hewitt	1936–40		
Billy Voisey	1940–4	England	1
Jack Cock	1944–8	England	2
Charlie Hewitt	1948–56		
Ron Gray	1956–8		
Jimmy Seed	1958–9	England	5
J.R. 'Reg' Smith	1959–61	England	2
Ron Gray	1961–3		
Billy Gray	1963–6		
Benny Fenton	1966–74		
Gordon Jago	1974–7		
George Petchey	1978–80		
Peter Anderson	1980–2		
George Graham	1982–6	Scotland	12
John Docherty	1986–90		
Bruce Rioch	1990–2	Scotland	24
Mick McCarthy	1992–6	R. of Ireland	57
Jimmy Nicholl	1996–7	N. Ireland	73
John Docherty	1997		
Billy Bonds	1997–8		
Keith Stevens	1998–00		
Alan McLeary	1999–00		
Mark McGhee	2000–3	Scotland	2
Dennis Wise	2003–5	England	21
Steve Claridge	2005		
Colin Lee	2005		
Dave Tuttle	2006		
Nigel Spackman	2006		
Willie Donnachie	2006–7	Scotland	35
Kenny Jackett	2007–	Wales	31

SECONDS OUT

The only boxing bout to take place at the New Den came on 19 March 1994 between London-born Michael Bentt, now resident in the USA and Norwich-based Herbie Hide, who fought for the WBO World Heavyweight Championship. Bentt lost his title to Hide by a knockout in the seventh of a 12-round contest. Such were his injuries that Bentt was forced to retire, after just a 13-fight career. Michael Bentt went on to become a film actor.

A SOLDIER'S TALE – PART ONE

Tommy Hyslop, a private in the 2nd Battalion Scots Guards, was on a furlough (leave), ostensibly for a visit back to his native Scotland, when he chose to renew his acquaintance with Millwall Athletic. He'd already played in the FA Cup tie against Woolwich Arsenal the previous November, and was now in the Millwall team to play West Bromwich Albion – under the name 'Willing' – for the last match at the end of April 1893.

Such was his was passion for the game and, not realising or caring that the Army Football Association had recently passed new regulations preventing serving soldiers joining the ranks of professional clubs (at the time Millwall were not a pro club, but were in the process of changing their status), Tommy happily went on to help Millwall gain a 1–0 victory.

Unfortunately, a whisper of his involvement in a match had arrived back at headquarters; a detachment under the command of Quartermaster-Sergeant Murray went in search of him, firstly to the Arsenal who were due to play Stoke. However, failing to locate Tom at Plumstead, the party headed for the East Ferry Road. Arriving while play was in progress, Murray waited patiently until its finish before Tom was arrested and returned to Wellington Barracks under escort.

This caper would prevent Tom from retiring from the Army for two years, but when he finally left the forces he would go on to play for Sunderland, Stoke and Glasgow Rangers among others, and was capped on two occasions by Scotland in 1896. Despite his blip with the military, Tom returned to the colours in 1901 to serve in the Boer War. Another little-known fact about him was his real surname was not Hyslop, but Bryce-Scoullar.

SEE YOU, JIMMY

Given Millwall's Scottish origins, how is this for a tartan eleven who have served the Lions?

1.	Malcolm Finlayson	(1947–56)
2.	Alex Jardine	(1950–8)
3.	David Storrier	(1902–4)
4.	Tommy Brown	(1946–9)
5.	Tommy Wilson	(1960–8)
6.	Jimmy Forsyth	(1929–39)
7.	Martin Moran	(1902–4)
8.	Alex Rae	(1990–6)
9.	Billy Hunter	(1904–9)
10.	Hugh Curran	(1963–6)
11.	Billy Neil	(1963–72)

Manager: Bob Hunter (1918–33)

FOREIGN CLIMES

The Lions have not been the most avid tourists like some clubs, but they have managed a few trips overseas, with their first sojourn occurring in May 1911. Millwall and London rivals Clapton Orient had been invited to contest the Dubonnet Cup in Paris. The concept of the match was seen as a missionary role to introduce the professional game to the French. But Millwall's 3–0 loss, their general play and overall approach hardly endeared them to locals.

There were also two trips to Rotterdam either side of the Second World War that both ended in defeats. The first was a 3–1 loss to a Dutch FA XI in November 1935 and then another against the same opposition in September 1947, where the Dutch ran riot to win 9–3. It was 20 years before Millwall ventured to Holland again, but this time their two-match tour saw them beat Go Ahead Eagles 2–0 and then draw with Sparta Rotterdam 1–1. In between, and following promotion, the Lions went to West Germany in 1962 only to suffer a pair of defeats, 2–1 at Hamborn 07 and 5–1 at TuS Neuendorf.

An enterprising tour of Sweden took place in 1978 which saw the Lions unbeaten in four matches, with a 1–0 victory over IFK Mora, two 3–0 successes, over Vasteras SK and Horfors IAF, and a 1–1 draw against Kramfors.

A flying visit to play a return game against Swiss team Servette also finished 1–1 in September 1989. A month later the Lions flew off to the Channel Islands to face a Jersey FA XI whom they beat 2–0. Prior to this, in May of that year, Millwall had really pushed the boat out when they undertook a two-match tour to Western Australia. It was a just reward for players' efforts after finishing in tenth place in their first ever season in Division One. Both fixtures were played in Perth and resulted in wins over Western Australia 1–0, and then Perth Italia 3–0.

There was a rash of tours to Ireland in the 1990s before an arranged tour of Germany was nearly aborted in 2001, when games against Eintracht Frankfurt and FSV Mainz were cancelled owing to the threat of violence. The Lions did manage to find a German amateur team to play, SV Weingarten, in which Marc Bircham scored the game's only goal.

A trip to Sweden and Norway took place in 2002 with matches against GAIS in Gothenburg that finished goalless before Norwegian side Tistedalen were beaten 2–1. The tour was rounded off with a win in Sweden, 2–0 over Trollhättan.

Following their first FA Cup final in 2004, Millwall made a three-match tour to Canada. They took on Team Canada, only to lose 1–0, before defeating a Vancouver all-star side (VMSL) 2–1. This was followed by a 1–1 draw against fellow tourists, the Scottish club Hearts.

Norway was again Millwall's destination in July 2005 under Steve Claridge's short tenure as manager when they visited FK Lyn of Oslo, who beat the Lions 3–0. The second match was a 3–2 success against FK Orn Horten. The following year, 2006, saw a first ever visit to Iceland with two matches taking place in the capital, Reykjavik. A 2–0 defeat came against Thróttur and was followed by a 4–0 drubbing at the hands of the KR club who scored all their goals in the first-half.

THE FIRST CLOSED CIRCUIT GAME

When Millwall visited Workington on Friday 28 January 1966 for a vital Third Division fixture, it would be the first transmission of its kind to be beamed back live to London. The attendance at The Den for the broadcast was 9,174 who paid £3,450 for the privilege – it was more than double the official gate at Workington, which was 4,323.

Sportscast, the company who staged the event, were more than satisfied to make a 'small profit' and the atmosphere created by the crowd was just as good as if they were watching the real thing. Although at times the reception on the four 30ft screens dipped in quality, the fans did not seem to mind as they cheered, booed and clapped their way through the 90 minutes, despite the game finishing 0–0.

AN FA CUP FINAL

FA Cup finals are not usually meant for clubs like Millwall, but on 22 May 2004 they finally broke their duck to appear in world's most famous knockout competition when they faced one of England's most honour-laden clubs, Manchester United. The result, a 3–0 win for United, was not unexpected, least of all by the Millwall support who were proud just to attend a landmark in the club's history. The icing on the Lions' cake was added when Curtis Weston became the youngest player at 17 years 119 days to appear in a final when he replaced player-manager Dennis Wise.

Their path to the Millennium Stadium final had been tinged with a fair amount of good fortune and would see them uncannily draw four teams they had never faced in the competition before. Walsall at home was followed by a trip to Telford United in the fourth round. Then Burnley were beaten at home, and the Lions drew Tranmere Rovers, also at the New Den. After defeating Rovers in the replay they then, ironically, faced Sunderland, who had been the Lions' 1937 conquerors at Old Trafford in what was Millwall's fourth semi-final (the others had been in 1900, 1903 and 1937).

The Lions route to the final was thus:

Third round	Walsall (H)	2–1
		Braniff, Cahill
Fourth round	Telford United (A)	2–0
		Ifill, Wise
Fifth round	Burnley (H)	1–0
		Dichio
Sixth round	Tranmere Rovers (H)	0–0
Sixth round replay	Tranmere Rovers (A)	2–1
		Cahill, Harris
Semi-final	Sunderland (N)	1–0
		Cahill

THE LOWEST GATES

The lowest attendances in modern times at The Den for a competitive first-team fixture came for the visit of West Bromwich Albion in the first round of the Full Members' Cup in October 1986, when just 967 hardy souls saw Millwall ease through 2–0, thanks to goals from Teddy Sheringham and John Leslie.

Despite finishing in ninth place in 1981/82, Millwall experienced their two lowest Football League attendances at Cold Blow Lane within a fortnight of each other. They occurred in the latter stages of the campaign for the midweek matches against Plymouth Argyle and Chesterfield. Argyle's visit attracted just 2,562 spectators and was bettered, but only just (by 103 extra fans), when Chesterfield appeared before 2,665 supporters.

THE BIG TEN HOME ATTENDANCES

The top ten attendances at The Den (Cold Blow Lane) have all come in FA Cup ties bar, one, with three of them coming in the magnificent run of 1936/37.

1	48,762	v Derby County	20 February 1937
2	45,646	v Newcastle United	26 January 1957
3	45,642	v Notts County	23 October 1948*
4	42,474	v Manchester City	4 February 1937
5	44,250	v Middlesbrough	19 February 1927
6	42,595	v Birmingham City	10 February 1957
7	42,250	v Swansea Town	20 February 1926
8	42,170	v Fulham	27 January 1951
9	41,503	v Chelsea	30 January 1937
10	41,260	v Tottenham Hotspur	28 January 1967

* Division Three South

THE OLDEST LION

Right-back Jack Fort could well hold the record for being the oldest player to turn out for Millwall, which he did against Bristol City at The Den on 7 December 1929, at the tender age of 41 years and 236 days. A marvellous defender and a great clubman, he was a month past his 33rd birthday when he gained his only England cap in 1921 against Belgium, who were coached by former Lion Willie Maxwell at the time.

Another two former England internationals also feature as Millwall's oldest debutants. Ray Wilkins was 40 years and 115 days old when he appeared against Colchester United in January 1997, while goalkeeper Nigel Spink made his first start for the Lions against Northampton Town at the age of 39 years and 50 days.

The other veteran who comes close to the other three is centre-half Arthur Whalley who played eight times for Millwall in the 1924/25 season. He was 38 years and 248 days old when made his debut at Gillingham in October 1924.

ANYONE SEEN MY BOOTS?

An event took place in the summer of 1904 when, at Thames Police Court on 12 July, a young man named William Evans was remanded on a charge of stealing and receiving a pair of football boots, which had been stolen from Millwall's North Greenwich ground.

It all began a month earlier when the groundsman discovered that the pavilion had been broken into, with four shirts and a pair of boots (John McLean's) missing. On a Monday afternoon shortly afterwards, the groundsman, probably Elijah Moor, saw a young lad wearing the boots (he turned out to be Evans' brother) and the police were duly informed.

When Evans was arrested at Bridge Street, Cubitt Town, he stated that he found the boots on the Thames foreshore, and then later said they had been given to him by a man. At the hearing his brother was called and said the prisoner had given him the boots at the beginning of July. The stipendiary magistrate, Mr Cluer, remanded Evans to give the police an opportunity of tracing the shirts.

Scottish centre-half John McLean spent three very consistent seasons with Millwall from 1903 to 1906 after signing from Bristol Rovers. But during his time at North Greenwich he became renowned for leaving his main accoutrement for playing the game, his football boots, carelessly lying about in the pavilion.

LIONS ON THE ROCK

When the Football Association sent a squad to play Gibraltar in April 1973, two of their members were Lions – Bryan King (goalkeeper) and defender Dennis Burnett, a just reward for their sterling service to Millwall over the previous six seasons. Both of them came on for the whole of the second half to replace two participants of England's 1966 World Cup-winning team, Gordon Banks and Nobby Stiles. The FA XI won 9–0. Also in the team that day was Les Barrett who went on to sign for the Lions in 1978.

THE BLIND LION

Some time in the early 1920s, Millwall's long-standing director George Saunders issued instructions to members of the staff that if a suitable model Lion was seen by anyone, they were to buy it. So, when passing a stonemason's yard in Walthamstow, Lions skipper Len Graham spotted the ideal specimen and promptly purchased it.

Leo was instantly erected with due pomp and on the following Saturday, Millwall unexpectedly lost at home. Following the game George immediately sought out Len and, pointing to the Lion, said, 'For God's sake take that ****** thing back. It's got its ****** eyes shut!'

THE WELSH WONDER

When Welsh centre-forward Wally Davis, height 5ft 7in, signed for Millwall in November 1911, he was accompanied by another new signing, outside-right Teddy Bassett who measured in at 5ft 5in. After the formalities had been completed, the pair were seen by director Tom Thorne who commented on how small both the new acquisitions were. Quick as a flash, Wally replied, 'Yes sir and you are paying us according to size too.'

Wally was a phenomenal footballer who in 142 games for the Lions amassed 91 goals. He scored arguably one of Millwall's most amazing goals, against Bradford City in a FA Cup tie in January 1914, a goal that Billy 'Banger' Voisey described as the best he had ever seen and about which the press went into overdrive in their graphic descriptions. He was awarded five caps for Wales before the First World War, but while playing football for his Army unit in Italy, Wal sustained an injury that forced his retirement from the game.

He was the son of Alderman D.J. Davis who became Mayor of West Ham for 1920/21. Sadly Wally was never to reach old age – he was found drowned in Bow Creek in May 1937 at the age of 48.

OI, REF!

Before he became an eminent football administrator, Sir Stanley Rous had been a Football League referee between 1927 and 1934. He was officiating at a match at The Den between Millwall and Charlton, when he assumed an outfield player had punched the ball away from danger. Rous immediately blew his whistle and awarded a penalty-kick.

As the bewildered players rose and began to untangle themselves, they gave Rous a quizzical look. It was then that he (Rous) realised it was the goalkeeper who had cleared the ball and not a defender. Deciding to brazen out his faux pas, he calmly walked to the side of the pitch to bellow at the crowd, 'If the man with the whistle blows it again I will have him removed!' He restarted the game with a dropped ball, thereby hiding any further embarrassment.

Another story attributed to him, and it could have been in the same match, was that Rous had been the victim of much sarcasm from one particular fan. Fed up with constant barracking, he promptly stopped the game to confront his tormentor, enquiring, 'Who's refereeing this game?' The instant put-down was 'Neither of us!' It left Rous rather speechless.

Sir Stanley went on to become the Secretary of the Football Association and later President of FIFA.

SUNDAY BEST

The first Football League match to take place on a Sunday was staged at The Den on 20 January 1974 when Millwall entertained Fulham. It kicked-off at 11.30 a.m., in front of 15,340 spectators, the biggest turnout of the season so far. To get around the legal aspects of playing on the Sabbath, the fans, to gain entrance, had to purchase the match programme, as no money could be taken through the turnstiles. Millwall won a closely fought derby encounter with the historic first goal (and only one of the match) being scored by Brian Clark after just 4 minutes. It ended a barren run of seven matches without a win.

THE LION WHO NEARLY BECOME A BEE

One club's loss is another's gain and a perfect example is when Millwall signed up inside-forward Johnny Shepherd, a.k.a. 'Shep'. This would not have been the case had Brentford's coach at the time, George Poyser, taken the advice of a fellow member of staff. However, the reluctant Poyser, on watching John's performance one Sunday afternoon, decided to go against his colleague's assessment, with a dismissive remark of 'I don't like a player who stands with his hands on hips during a match.' When his opinion on Shepherd went unheeded, the coach eventually left Brentford for a job at The Den, and following his arrival he mentioned John to his old friend Ron Gray, and as they say the rest is history.

How Brentford must have rued their coach's opinion when John, on his Lions debut, hit all the Millwall goals in a 4–1 victory (still the only Lions player to achieve this) at Leyton Orient in October 1952. John would score 82 goals in 172 matches, which includes a Millwall record of 15 goals in 17 FA Cup appearances. His four hat-tricks in his initial season of 1952/53 all came before the turn of the year, not bad for a lad who had once suffered Infantile Paralysis (Polio).

CONSPIRACY!

When Millwall lost their FA Cup semi-final against Sunderland at Huddersfield in 1937, there began the post-match rumblings from the Lions fans of bias against them by the Football Association, such as the location of the match, the performance of the northern referee, and the flawed allocation of tickets. However, the main gripes had been the award of two dodgy free-kicks to Sunderland that enabled them to come from behind to win 2–1, and the failure to award a penalty to Millwall. The theory was that the FA never wanted a Third Division team in their final.

LIONS ON THE BIG SCREEN

Other than their coverage on the television, Millwall or their players have been featured on the big screen, with former player Jack Cock appearing in two films. The first was a silent picture of 1920, *The Winning Goal,* and a decade later he played Jim Blake, a footballer in *The Great Game,* one of the first films to feature football as the main topic. It also included an aspiring actor named Rex Harrison.

After the Second World War, a film called *Small Town Story* was released in 1953 which had a football thread running through it and would use players from Millwall and Arsenal. It starred Donald Houston and Kent Walton who later became a TV sports presenter. The film's editing had been processed by a gent named George Fisher, the same name as one of Millwall's legend who appeared in the picture.

Frank Peterson had a bit part in the film version of *Porridge* in the 1979. In the 1981 film *Escape to Victory* former Millwall outside-left Kevin O'Callaghan (then of Ipswich Town) played the part of Tony Lewis, an Irish goalkeeper (talk about miscasting), and who would have his thunder stolen by Sylvester Stallone.

RED MIST

Sendings-off are a fairly regular occurrence these days, with a proliferation of red cards, some of which seem totally unwarranted. The holder of the unwanted record of most dismissals for Millwall is Alan Dunne with seven, while the very combative pair of Keith Stevens and Alex Rae have six dismissals each. The opponents who Millwall have had most players sent-off against are Bristol Rovers, with a staggering total of ten. In fact, Welsh centre-half Brian Law managed it twice against them in 1997/98.

The Lions' red card records in 1989/90 was just two and they were both given to another centre-back, when the unfortunate Steve Wood was ushered off against Stoke and Norwich. Scott Fitzgerald, Gerard Lavin and Tim Cahill were three who were given the heave-ho at Gillingham in 1998 while Millwall's desperate relegation season of 2005/06 was aptly summed up with a record 14 red cards. In the match at Burnley, players Ben May, Jody Morris and goalkeeper Andy Marshall were another trio to upset an overzealous referee.

During 2000/01 Millwall were reduced to nine men in three matches against Wycombe, Ipswich and Bristol City. Canadian international Marc Bircham saw double red in two cup ties at Bristol City in the FA Cup and Auto Windscreens competition that saw City won both games 1–0 in 1997/98.

The seven Millwall red cards received during the 2010/11 season came against clubs whose title ended with the suffix 'City'. Darren Carter and Steve Morison saw red against Bristol City, while Neil Harris' sending-off at Coventry came within two minutes of him coming on as a substitute. Alan Dunne, along with loanee Jens Berthel Askou, upset the referee in the two games with Leicester. Lastly, Liam Trotter (away) and Alan Dunne (home) also displeased the match official in the Cardiff fixtures.

TOP O' THE MORNIN'

Millwall have been fortunate to acquire some very talented footballers from the Emerald Isle and here is a team that the fans could be justifiably proud of.

1.	David Forde	(2008–)
2.	Kenny Cunningham	(1989–94)
3.	Robbie Ryan	(1997–2004)
4.	Ray Brady	(1957–62)
5.	Charlie Hurley	(1953–7)
6.	Pat Saward	(1951–4)
7.	Dave Savage	(1994–8)
8.	Mark Kennedy	(1992–4)
9.	Richard Sadlier	(1996–2003)
10.	Eamon Dunphy	(1965–73)
11.	Joe Haverty	(1962–64)

LET 'EM COME

As Roy Green's Millwall anthem boldly states, 'Let 'em come', and after 84 seasons of being members of the Football League, Millwall have met 110 different clubs in the league and have defeated all of them bar two, Arsenal and Liverpool.

The other teams to have played League football but who have never met the Lions are Bootle, Boston United, Burton Albion, Burton Wanderers, Darwen, Durham City, Gainsborough Trinity, Glossop North End, Middlesbrough Ironopolis, Maidstone United, Morecambe, Nelson, New Brighton, Northwich Victoria, Scarborough, Stalybridge Celtic and Stevenage.

The Lions have opposed past and present members like Ashington, Barnet, Burton United, Dagenham & Redbridge, Kidderminster Harriers, Loughborough Town, Rushden & Diamonds and Thames in various competitions down through the years.

FA CUP SEMIS

Besides reaching their first FA Cup final in 2004, which is highlighted elsewhere in this book, Millwall have reached three other semis in their history.

The first occurred in 1900 when they were beaten by fellow Southern League side Southampton 3–0 following a 0–0 draw. This was followed three years later in 1903 with another 3–0 defeat, this time at the hands of Derby County at Villa Park. Millwall, in 1937, became the first Third Division club to reach such a stage before succumbing 2–1 to Sunderland, the then current Football League champions.

BOGEY GROUNDS

Every team, at any level of football, has any number of bogey grounds, with Haigh Avenue, Southport, being one of Millwall's. In six visits there, including an FA Cup tie, the Lions have failed to secure a victory. The five fixtures there in the Fourth Division between 1958 and 1964 saw the Lions lose 2–1, 1–0, 4–1 and 3–1. The only point Millwall earned at the Lancashire ground came with a 0–0 draw in 1964/65 (even then Southport failed to score a penalty). The cup tie back in 1930/31 was also lost 3–1.

However, the Haigh Avenue experience pales into insignificance when compared to Sydenham, home of Crystal Palace for a while and the old venue of the FA Cup finals, where Millwall, in eleven visits, have recorded just one victory. The full record is:

24/3/1900	Southampton	0–0	FA Cup semi-final
17/11/1906	Crystal Palace	0–1	Southern League
21/3/1908	Crystal Palace	0–2	Southern League
21/11/1908	Crystal Palace	1–2	Southern League
12/3/1910	Crystal Palace	1–4	Southern League
25/3/1911	Crystal Palace	0–1	Southern League
8/4/1912	Crystal Palace	0–3	Southern League
26/12/1912	Crystal Palace	0–2	Southern League
3/1/1914	Crystal Palace	0–3	Southern League
26/12/1914	Crystal Palace	1–0	Southern League
11/1/1930	Corinthians	2–2	FA Cup third round

DIVISION THREE SOUTH CUP

With its Northern counterpart, the trophy was inaugurated in the 1933/34 campaign, but following relegation from Division Two in 1934, Millwall became eligible the following season. They made their bow at home to Brighton & Hove Albion in October 1934 with a 2–1 success. However, any thoughts of winning the title were crushed with a 5–0 hammering at Exeter City in round three. A 1–0 loss at The Den to Coventry City ended the Lions' hopes of further glory in 1935/36.

Millwall's run to the final occurred the following season (1936/37) with victories over Walsall at home 5–2 (five different scorers) in round one, before Clapton Orient were defeated 3–2, also at The Den. A two-legged affair in the semi-final against Torquay United saw the Lions enter the final after a 2–2 draw in Devon before a thumping 5–0 home victory. Millwall met Watford in a two-legged final. Following the two matches, the final was left undecided when the scores finished 3–3 on aggregate. Both Watford and Millwall would share the trophy for six months each.

The Lions' final season in the competition came in 1937/38; they again reached the semi-final, following wins over Gillingham at The Den, 4–0, and 2–1 at Swindon Town. However, the format had been changed regarding the semi-final with just one game to decide who went through. Unfortunately it was not the Lions, who went out following a 2–0 defeat at Bristol City. The competition was mothballed following its last appearance in 1945/46.

Dave Mangnall was Millwall's leading goalscorer in the tournament with six, including a hat-trick against Gillingham; Jack Thorogood was another three-goal hero in the 5–0 romp over Torquay.

The Den was the venue for the Southern section final between Bristol Rovers and Watford in 1934/35, which Rovers won 3–2 on 15 April 1935.

TWENTIETH-CENTURY BOY

When Brentford scored in the 85th minute to take a 2–1 lead at The Den in Millwall's last match of 1999 (on 28 December), not even their most fervent fan would have given them a chance of taking anything from the game, which they had dominated. However, an 89th-minute equaliser from 87th-minute substitute Paul Shaw set up a frantic finish that no one could have envisaged.

Enter Dave Livermore, Millwall's battling midfield player, who would provide the sting in the tail to a storming derby match that had had many twists and turns during its duration. David had only been on the pitch since the 82nd minute, having replaced Tim Cahill, when, in a dramatic turn of events, he thrashed home Neil Harris' low cross deep into injury time for the winner. There's nothing too unusual in that, many games have been settled like this.

However, the league's sponsors, Nationwide, had decided to present specially commissioned awards to the scorer of the last goal of the twentieth century and to the first in the twenty-first. Millwall's match with Brentford had been delayed for ten minutes due to a larger than usual crowd. The start at 15.10 would guarantee a late finish, and when David scored the winner it was timed at 17.02. However, there was a rival for the award in Chris Priest of Macclesfield Town who had also scored an injury-time goal – the delay at Moss Rose had been caused by an accident on the M6.

Following the league's adjudication, David's goal was deemed to be the final goal of the century and he was presented with his prize as the 'Millennium Man' before the home game against Stoke City in January 2000.

AN UNUSUAL REQUEST

As requests go, a bribe to win a game is most odd – it is usually offered for a team to lose. But this was the case when put to a pair of Millwall players just before Christmas 1918. A bookmaker from East Dulwich named Henry Thatcher – alias G. Wilson of Lordship Lane – approached inside-forward Dougie Thomson and defender Dick Griffiths to make sure the Lions WON their encounter with Brentford on 14 December at The Den. The two players had been fairly regular performers with the Lions that season while combining playing with their other jobs, Thomson with the Canadian pay office and Griffiths who, like so many of the club's supporters, was employed by the Port of London Authority.

Thomson had been visited by Thatcher, a complete stranger to Doug, at his home the day before the game, and related to him that he had been sent by a friend, and that he (Thomson) was a decent chap. Thatcher added he had been offered the not-so-generous odds of 5/4 against Millwall and thought he should pay a visit to Doug just to make sure the game was won. With that, Thatcher slipped a £1 note into Doug's pocket and promised a further £3 on Saturday night if the Lions either drew or were victorious.

Thatcher then went around to Griffiths' home in West Ham where he told him he had £50 on Millwall to win at 5/4. Offering the same deal to Dick as he had to Doug, £1 down with £3 to follow, Dick's reply was 'What's this for? We are always out to win. You people don't give money for nothing and if I take it you will come along again, wanting me to do something else.'

Following Millwall's 3–1 victory, in which Thomson scored one of the goals, both Doug and Dick went straight away to see the chairman Tom Thorne who in turn contacted the police. The next day (Sunday) Thatcher called on Thomson and left £3 with Doug's wife. On instructions from the police Thomson met Thatcher at Westminster underground station and after entering a nearby shop the bookmaker suggested a further wager, to include two other Millwall players for the forthcoming fixture against Chelsea, and if Millwall won or lost there would be £60 available to share between the four.

Under cross-examination at Bow Street Magistrates Court in January 1919, Thomson told the hearing the £15 was not an invention and as a result Thatcher was given three months' imprisonment. He successfully appealed the sentence which was reduced to a £50 fine plus £100 costs. Thatcher's train of thought was unbelievably naïve, in that he felt he was not doing anything wrong by offering financial inducements.

SUTCLIFFE UTTERS

Millwall's disappointing performance in 1903 in an FA Cup semi-final defeat to Derby County at Villa Park, in which most of the team played way below par, saw distraught goalkeeper John William Sutcliffe being asked to account for his failure to stop the first goal. The England international attributed it to an unpredictable wind and his sight being impaired by the spring sunshine.

Poor J.W. was again at fault for the Rams' second goal, and he found sympathy in short supply from the Millwall fans who had travelled up to Birmingham as they saw dreams of appearing in the final dashed for the second time in three years. However, he recovered to finish the season as Millwall's number one, but it came as no surprise when he left in the summer, citing the reason 'that he found East London uncongenial'.

JOHN 'TINY' JOYCE

'Tiny', ironically nicknamed because of his height and bulky frame, was a goalkeeping legend for Millwall having joined in 1900 from Southampton, but in fact would sign for the Lions on no less than three occasions during his career. He had spells with Blackburn Rovers and Tottenham Hotspur between his Millwall sojourns. He joined for the third and last time in 1915, playing until 1918, and was later appointed assistant trainer in 1919, a position he held until 1938.

During 1906 he contested a ball-kicking competition with Tom 'Pom-Pom' Whiting of Chelsea, which 'Tiny' won with a punt of 94 yards 2ft from a dead kick. Three years later, when playing for Spurs against Peterborough, he was also credited with some prodigious punching when one ball went to a distance of 76ft 2in.

Although football may no longer feature so highly in Tiny's surviving family now, he does have two great-grandsons, Mark and Ian Bostridge, who have taken on different vocations. Mark is an historian and Ian is a Classical singer and appears regularly at Covent Garden. John 'Tiny' Joyce died at Greenwich in 1956.

THE RIVER THAMES

Millwall's link to the River Thames, and the former docks and wharves along it, have long since passed, but the club still maintains a connection through a designated 'Docker's Day' match at New Den which is usually held in February, with the first being in 2007. Even a photograph showing a local stretch of the river used to adorn the cover of Millwall's match programme back in 1964.

When Bill Nelan, a Thames barge builder became a director in 1960, he named his constructions after Millwall players. The list below has been gleaned from old registers that listed not only Bill's craft, but all the other dumb barges operating on the river. The register is part of the archive of the Museum in Docklands.

Alex Stepney	*Jim Seed*
Billy Gray	*Jimmy Jinks*
Brian Snowdon	*Joe Broadfoot*
Charlie Hurley	*Joe Haverty*
Dave Harper	*John Gilghrist*
Harry Cripps	*John Summers*
J.R. Smith	*Pat Saward*
Jack Fort	

These barges were managed by W.T. Beaumont & Sons Ltd, while three others, named the *Ray Brand*, *Ron Gray* and *Millwall* were run by other companies.

A DOUBLE WHAMMY

Millwall signed Middlesbrough goalkeeper Ben Roberts on loan in February 1999; he would go on to keep goal for the Lions when they made their first appearance at Wembley for 54 years when they faced Wigan Athletic in the final of the Auto Windscreens Shield later that year. Ben had already played at Wembley for Middlesbrough in the 1997 FA Cup final against Chelsea in which he was beaten after just 43 seconds by Roberto Di Matteo, the fastest goal in a Wembley final at the time. However, Ben was to suffer again, with only seconds remaining, he would be beaten when Paul Rogers claimed Wigan's winner, as extra time beckoned.

MALTESE AFFECTION

Some time during the 1937/38 season Millwall received a letter from the secretary of Cospicua Lions, a club based in Malta seeking permission from the club, whether it would be appropriate if they could use the word 'Lions' in their title. The Maltese request was readily agreed to by manager Charlie Hewitt and in return, Millwall received a team photo of Cospicua Lions that went on to adorn the Millwall boardroom at The Den.

HOW MANY CAPS YOU GOT?

When goalkeeper David Forde came on as a 71st-minute substitute for the Republic of Ireland against Northern Ireland in late May 2011 for his first international appearance, he became the forty-eighth Millwall player to be awarded a full cap. Surprisingly, for all their early Caledonian connections, Millwall still await their first full Scottish international. The full list is as follows:

England (8)

H.E. Banks	1	F.S. Fox	1
J.W. Sutcliffe	1	R.H. Hill	1
J. Fort	1	H. Roberts	1
L. Graham	2	J.R. Smith	2

Wales (8)

J. Davies	1	S.R. Lowndes	6
A.E. Watkins	3	S.J. Lovell	5
R. Jones	2	M. Allen	5
W.O. Davis	5	S. Morison	7

N. Ireland (6)

T.H. Brolly	4	B. Hamilton	4
E.G. Hinton	2	A.G. Rogan	1
W.J. McCullough	1	J. McQuoid	2

Republic of Ireland (12)

P. Saward	1	G. Waddock	2
C. Hurley	1	J.F. Byrne	1
J. Haverty	6	D.T. Savage	5
E. Dunphy	22	R.T. Sadlier	1
A. Cascarino	15	S.J. Reid	7
M. McCarthy	19	D. Forde	1

Australia (5)

D.S. Mitchell	1	K.V. Muscat	3
J. Van Blerk	4	T. Cahill	4
L. Neill	10		

Barbados (2)

M.E. Gilkes	6	P. Ifill	2

USA (2)

J.J. Kerr	4	K. Keller	16

Canada (3)

M. Bircham	13	J. Simpson	13
A.R. Serioux	9		

St Kitts & Nevis (1)		**Comoros (1)**	
B. Bowry	2	N. Abdou	1

THERE'S ALWAYS ONE

Wit and humour abound at football grounds and The Den (both versions) is no different. One comment that made former Lions goalkeeper Malcolm Finlayson laugh came when the German War Crimes Tribunals were still fresh in the memories of many people. Finlayson and the rest of the team were coming out for the second half following a losing and desperate first 45 minutes when a wag in the crowd yelled 'They hanged the wrong bloody eleven at Nuremburg!' Malcolm was still chuckling when he took up his position.

THE £50,000 FORWARD LINE

Millwall faced a dearth of goals in the first two seasons following their entry into the Football League in 1920, with just 80 goals in 84 games. In an attempt to alleviate the problem (as the story that grew into a legend goes), Millwall supposedly made an offer for the entire Raith Rovers forward line during the 1922/23 season. The amount was, a mammoth (at the time) £50,000 for the five players – Bell, Miller, Jennings, Archibald and the marvellous Alex James. The truth, however, came to light some years later when Millwall director John Beveridge gave an interview to a newspaper. He stated that he and manager Bob Hunter, both Scots, had 'spoofed' the overture, with Beveridge stating that 'Millwall hadn't a bean at the time and there was no mention of pounds sterling.' Beveridge went on to add, 'In fact the "cash" was a fifty-thousand German Mark note,' a memento he acquired for less than one new penny after the First World War.

Long after the Raith Rovers story had passed into Millwall folklore the mention of another multi-bid came when a report appeared in the press following Millwall's FA Cup tie against Northampton Town in 1945. The Lions, the media had stated, had been so impressed with certain players in the Cobblers team, there was supposedly an offer of a five-figure sum for a number of them, plus a separate bid for centre-forward Alf Morrall. The speculation brought back the memories to the older Lions fans of the Raith story and like the earlier sensation, there was no substance in it, as none of those Northampton players ever arrived at The Den. The coincidence of these fables is that they both followed in the aftermath of a world war when times were austere and money for such frivolity would be hard to find.

UPS AND DOWNS

After 84 seasons of Football League membership, Millwall have managed ten promotions and eight relegations. The successes are as follows:

1927/28 to Division Two	1975/76 to Division Two
1933/38 to Division Two	1984/85 to Division Two
1961/62 to Division Three	1987/88 to Division One
1964/65 to Division Three	2000/01 to League One
1965/66 to Division Two	2009/10 to League One

The failures are:

1933/34 to Division Three South	1978/79 to Division Three
1947/48 to Division Three South	1989/90 to Division Two
1963/64 to Division Four	1995/96 to Division Three
1974/75 to Division Three	2005/06 to League One

WEMBLEY

Like Haig Avenue and the old cup final ground at Sydenham, Millwall's visits to the national stadium, in north-west London were not very happy affairs. Eventually, the ghost of failure was finally laid to rest in 2010 with the Lions' first victory at Wembley in four visits. The Wembley record is:

7/4/1945
    v Chelsea   Football League South final   Lost 2–0

18/4/1999
    v Wigan Athletic   Auto Windscreens Shield final   Lost 1–0

24/5/2009
    v Scunthorpe Utd League play-off final   Lost 3–2

29/5/2010
    v Swindon Town   League play-off final   Won 1–0

IN THE WAR

When competitive football was suspended in September 1939, it would be replaced by regional leagues, which meant shorter travelling distances for matches, and through the guest system clubs could utilise players from other teams. Leagues would have different titles, but in Millwall's case the main one was Football League South which, along with a cup competition, would be the staple diet over the course of the war's duration.

The Lions took some terrible hammerings during this time – 10–0 from the Arsenal in early 1941, two Chelsea victories of 8–0 and 7–0, and Fulham also smashed in another seven without reply. However, one of only six victories in 1942/43 was the remarkable scoreline at Luton Town when Millwall won 11–3. It was their only 'double' of the season, having beaten the Hatters 5–1 at Charlton's Valley ground, The Den having been put out of use by enemy action.

Continuing with the war theme; when Millwall set off to play Arsenal at White Hart Lane (Arsenal Stadium had been requisitioned) in January 1945, the trip to Tottenham's ground had to be completed by lorry. The team's charabanc (coach/bus) broke down, and it was only the kindness of a passing lorry driver who told the players to pile aboard with their kit, that got the team to the ground. The Lions lost the match 4–1 after holding a one-goal lead for over an hour before Arsenal's guest, Stanley Matthews, took matters in hand to turn the game in the Gunners' favour.

HAT-TRICKS

Since Millwall became a professional club in 1894 a total of 159 hat-tricks (3 or more goals) have been scored by the men in blue, with one 6, four 5s, twenty-three 4s and 131 trebles. Welshman Joe Davies hit the 6 when Wolverton were overwhelmed 9–1 in October 1897, while three of the 5-goal hauls came in the Southern League days. Jack Calvey was responsible for two of them, one against the luckless Wolverton, who were swamped 12–0 (eleven months before Davies went one better). Jack's other victims were Luton Town who were beaten 6–2 in the United League.

Alf Twigg was at the forefront with 5 goals when Millwall annihilated Watford 10–1 in the first game of January 1907. This feat has only been matched once in the Football League when Dick Parker hit his 5 against Norwich City on the opening day of the 1926/27 season. Mind you, Teddy Sheringham did manage 5 goals in the game against Plymouth Argyle at The Den in February 1991, 4 for the Lions, and an own goal in a 4–1 win.

The player, who has registered the most hat-tricks is Jack Calvey with eight, closely followed by Neil Harris on seven, and Sheringham with five. Lion Gary Townend's two hat-tricks both came away from home, with a treble in a 5–1 success at Darlington in April 1962 and all the goals in a 3–1 win at Luton Town in December 1963.

The excellent Keith Weller scored one of the quickest hat-tricks, in just eight minutes (his only one for the club), against Bolton

Wanderers at The Den in August 1968. His strikes in the 38th, 40th, and 46th minutes (his last a penalty) secured a 3–1 success. Two other Lions could also claim the fastest hat-trick, with Peter Burridge scoring four against Chester in January 1961, with three coming in the 44th, 47th and 51st minutes. Previously, Johnny Shepherd had hit four on his debut at Leyton Orient in October 1952 – following his first on 23 minutes, his other three goals arrived in the 46th, 48th and 51st minutes.

The last rapid hat-trick was scored by Neil Harris in March 2009 with a threesome in 10 minutes at Hartlepool United, where Millwall overcame a 2-goal deficit to win 3–2. Millwall have never lost a match when a Lion has scored a hat-trick.

All four hat-tricks scored in 1926/27 were obtained by Dick Parker, while Michael Marks (at 18 years, 202 days) has been credited as the youngest Millwall hat-trick scorer, which he achieved in the 4–0 victory over Shrewsbury Town at The Den in October 1986.

Jason Puncheon of Southampton became the first loan player to score a hat-trick for Millwall in a 3–0 victory over Crystal Palace on 1 January 2011. It was also the first treble against Palace since Jack Thorogood's threesome at The Den in April 1936.

Neil Harris, Teddy Sheringham and John Shepherd have all scored six hat-tricks in competitive games for the Lions, while the 1920s super striker Dick Parker has five to his name. Dick's teammates Jack Cock and Johnny Landells claim four apiece as does Peter Burridge who plundered his goals in the early 1960s.

Back in the Southern League days John Calvey scored seven hat-tricks while the England international Bert Banks claimed four during his time with the club, and so did Alf Twigg.

HIGHS AND LOWS

The highest position Millwall have attained was tenth at the end of their initial season in the First Division of 1988/89. After beating QPR 3–2 on 1 October 1988 they headed the Division One table, and for a while were actually the top team in the Football League.

Millwall's nadir came in the 1949/50 campaign when they finished bottom of the pile in twenty-second in Division Three South, and then again in 1958 when they finished in twenty-third. These are the only two times the Lions have had seek to re-election to the Football League. Although Millwall were re-elected in 1958 with the highest number of votes, 46, it was a bitter-sweet situation for they were given a founder member place in the new Fourth Division, so in reality they had been 'relegated'.

THE CHAMPIONS

Millwall have been champions of a Football League division on five different occasions:

1927/28 Third Division South
Millwall won their first Football League championship in stunning style by scoring 127 goals and finishing ten points clear of runners-up Northampton Town. Losing only 5 matches out of 42 played, the Lions achieved their biggest victories in their history with 9–1 wins over both Torquay United and Coventry City. One defeat in the last dozen games confirmed their superiority, with three of the forward line amassing 85 goals between them.

1937/38 Third Division South
A decade would pass before Millwall obtained their second title, and again it was for the Third Division South. However, the race for promotion was a lot closer this time around with just one point separating the Lions and second-placed Bristol City. However, promotion was clinched on the last day with a superb 5–1 win at Exeter City.

1961/62 Fourth Division
The goalscoring prowess of Peter Burridge and Dave Jones had been seen the season before and Millwall were again to rely on this superb pair. Once more the Lions would nick it by a point,

with a disputed Burridge equaliser in the last game at Barrow. It gave them the point to overhaul Colchester United for first place following Accrington Stanley's resignation earlier in the season. Stanley's records were expunged, which saw the Lions lose two points and Colchester four, the Us having completed the double over them, and this was to prove vital in the final standings.

1987/88 Second Division
Millwall finally made it to the promised land of the First Division after a near miss in 1972. With the Lions making a substantial outlay in the transfer market during the summer by signing Tony Cascarino, George Lawrence, Steve Wood and former Lion Kevin O'Callaghan from Portsmouth, the expenditure was certainly justified by the final outcome. Despite a few blips along the way, it was a run of seven wins in the final eight games that decided the Second Division Championship was on its way to The Den for the first time.

2000/01 Division Two
Millwall were certainly the best team in the division and with three points for a win, the total of 93 was the highest in their history. The exploits of leading goalscorer Neil Harris and the emergence of both Tim Cahill and Steven Reid were vital cogs, but it was also the sound defence who contributed to a superb team effort. It included skipper Stuart Nethercott and the excellent goalkeeper Tony Warner who in no small way helped to claim another record by conceding just 11 goals at home.

CHARLIE'S TRUNK

When Charlie Burgess signed for Millwall in May 1898, after impressing with his native Montrose, he was met at King's Cross station by Bob Hunter, the Millwall trainer, who was to accompany Charlie back to his digs on the Isle of Dogs. Among his personal effects was a trunk that weighed a 'ton'. It required two porters, whose comments can only be imagined as they struggled to haul the trunk on to a carriage.

After negotiating the trip back to the island, Hunter was dying to know what the contents of the trunk were that made it so heavy. Once they were ensconced in Charlie's lodgings, the lid of the cumbersome piece of luggage was opened to finally satisfy Bob's curiosity. Much to Hunter's to surprise, Charlie's father had packed the trunk with a rather huge amount of potatoes, turnips and other root vegetables, because he was under the misconception that such eatables were scarce in London. Charlie spent two seasons with Millwall before joining Newcastle United in 1900. A big, strong and resolute full-back, he became a vital component in the team that reached FA Cup semi-final in 1900.

Charlie Burgess emmigrated to the United States in 1909, where he helped to transform the other passion in his life, golf, a sport that went on to become a national obsession with the Americans. Charlie went on to coach three golfing champions in Francis Quimet, Jesse Gifford and Ted Bishop, and was also instrumental in teaching the rudiments of the game to other American icons like the baseball player Babe Ruth and the crooner Bing Crosby. Charles Burgess passed away in May 1960 aged 86.

MATCH ABANDONDED

Fog had been the cause of abandonments in some of Millwall's early matches, with the combination of local domestic and factory pollutants and the ground's close proximity to the River Thames. The first meaningful game to fall foul of the weather was in December 1896 was the FA Cup tie against Sheppey United (which Millwall were winning 2–0), saw the referee to call a halt to proceedings at half time.

A similar occurrence came in another FA Cup fixture at The Den in January 1934 when the Lions were again leading by two goals, this time against Reading. A pea souper descended with just 15 minutes to go. Thankfully, Millwall won both these ties following replays.

Five weeks after the Sheppey FA Cup match, a Southern League encounter against Southampton in January 1897 was terminated with barely 15 minutes played. Heavy rain caused the stoppage with the score at 0–0 on this occasion. Precipitation was again the reason the Fourth Division match with Stockport County on Boxing Day 1959 was abandoned after 65 minutes, with the visitors leading 1–0. When the match was rearranged, Millwall ran out 3–2 winners.

Torrential rain forced the referee to stop the goalless match versus Sheffield United after 24 minutes on 12 September 1970. The fixture was hastily rearranged for Monday night, just over 48 hours later. During the weekend the weather had hardly improved and the conditions on the night seemed no better than on the Saturday. Fearing another postponement, the attendance of 5,363 reflected those fears, and the fans who did turn up must have wished they had hadn't bothered, given that the Lions lost 1–2.

As far the New Den is concerned, with its under-soil heating and excellent drainage, no game has yet had to be abandoned. The game against Swindon Town in 1994/95 was called off at a very late stage, though, owing to heavy and persistent rain. A second match to fall foul of the weather was the Barnsley fixture in December 2010. The pitch was fit for play at 12.00 p.m., but a sudden deluge of snow forced the match to be cancelled at around 12.15 p.m.

NEUTRAL GROUNDS

Apart from their four FA Cup semi-final venues, Millwall have occasionally been involved in deciding the outcome of games on neutral grounds, an action that will never take place again owing to the reorganisation of cup competition rules. The first instance for the Lions since joining the Football League came when they faced Northampton Town in a second replay in the third round at the Arsenal Stadium in January 1929.

Twelve months later they were asked to contest a second replay against the famous amateur club Corinthians at Chelsea's Stamford

Bridge. A Monday afternoon crowd of 58,775 saw Millwall advance to the next round 5–1.

A neutral venue was not to been seen on Millwall's horizon for another 45 years and then three came along in three consecutive seasons during the mid-1970s. In January 1975 the Lions lost in the FA Cup third round to Bury 0–2 at The Hawthorns, a ground at which Millwall had already lost a League Cup tie earlier in the season against West Brom.

Within the calendar year of 1975, Millwall were again asked to contest a second replay when they were taken to three games by non-league Yeovil Town. The tie was finally settled in Millwall's favour by Alan Hart's goal in the second half on a wintry December evening at Aldershot.

Following their 2–0 success at Highbury over Northampton Town in 1929, the Lions featured for a second time at Arsenal's famous old ground to face London rivals Orient, in October 1976. Millwall continued their winning run there with a result of 3–0, in what would only be the club's only League Cup tie to go to three meetings.

In the last campaign of the 1970s, season 1979/80, two FA Cup ties against non-league teams were, on police advice, switched to larger venues. In the first round Millwall defeated Salisbury 2–1 at The Dell, Southampton, which was followed by a trip to Selhurst Park in the second round, after being drawn away to Croydon. Something similar arose in November 2006 when Havant & Waterlooville were forced to cede home advantage when opposing the Lions in the FA Cup, by having to play the tie at Fratton Park, Portsmouth. Millwall won 2–1 on the day.

THEIR LOSS

When Millwall got promoted in 1938, there were many clubs in Division Three South who were none too pleased to see them go up, as their takings would suffer and for good reason. The reason for this is that in those days the away club would also take a share out of the home team's gate receipts.

The imbalance is remarkable and shows what an attraction Millwall were at the time. For instance Torquay United copped £181 from the Cold Blow Lane takings, whereas the Lions received a paltry £25 after their trip to Plainmoor. Likewise, Southend United coughed up a mere £67 for Millwall, but when they visited The Den they walked away with the princely sum of £245.

A MAN OF MANY TALENTS

Centre-forward Jack Cock became the final piece in the jigsaw when he was recruited from Plymouth Argyle in November 1927 to fill in for the injured Dick Park. Jack's haul of 25 goals in 27 matches justified manager Bob Hunter's decision to sign a player who was 34 and definitely in the veteran stage. But his goals and experience paved the way for Millwall to win their first ever promotion in 1928.

A former international, Jack made two appearances for England, and also served Huddersfield Town, Chelsea and Everton in a sparkling career. He saw service with the Footballers' Battalion in the First World War, during which he was reported, mistakenly as it turned out, to have been killed in action. He later became the recipient of the Military Medal.

His 77 league goals for the Lions remained a club record until Derek Possee passed it over 40 years later. Despite the rigours of war and football, Jack never lost his good looks and was the possessor of a fine tenor voice which he utilised on stage when football permitted. One tale told about him, when he was playing for Chelsea, was that in one particular match Jack had definitely left his shooting boots at home. Following another wayward effort the dissenting voice of a wit in the crowd shouted at the top of his voice, 'For goodness sake SING!'

After leaving the Lions, Jack wound down his career with Folkestone and later as a permit player with Walton & Hersham. It was around this time he appeared in a football-related film called *The Great Game,* which came ten years after his first starring role in the 1920 film *The Winning Goal*. He became Millwall's manager in 1944 and led them to their first Wembley appearance in the League South final against his old club Chelsea. Jack was in the hot seat until 1948 and later went on to become a publican in New Cross.

HERE TODAY, GONE TOMORROW

This old saying could not be more appropriate in relation to the untimely deaths of three Millwall trainers. The first of the triumvirate was Jimmy Lindsay in January 1897. Having put the players through their paces for the forthcoming FA Cup tie against Woolwich Arsenal, he engaged in some light-hearted boxing with skipper George King, when he suddenly collapsed and died on the spot.

How ironic that Jim's replacement, Bob Hunter, who arrived in the summer that year, would some 36 years later also meet his end while in office? Bob was to become an inspirational choice, especially when he became manager in 1918, by signing some of Millwall's greatest players like Jack Cock, Dick Parker and W.I. Bryant to name but three. Bob's sad demise on 29 March 1933 came four days after Millwall had beaten Charlton Athletic 4–1 at The Valley. Following his death, Bob's beloved Lions failed to win any of their remaining eight games, and had he lived, Millwall might have finished higher than their final place of seventh.

The last of a forlorn trilogy is Frank Jefferis, a former England international in his playing days who had appeared for both Everton and Preston, He had been engaged by Charlie Hewitt as part of his rebuilding scheme at The Den following Millwall's relegation in 1934. Frank had overseen Southport's best spell in their history as player-coach and then trainer-coach during the 1920s and would be seen as a vital acquisition to the Millwall coaching staff.

Frank was instrumental in the Lions reaching the FA Cup semi-final in 1937 and in the subsequent promotion to Division Two a year later. Then in May 1938, in the glow of glory, Frank Jefferis collapsed and died in the club's offices as he prepared to give a radio interview, having just been given an award.

Another sad loss in more recent times was the death of coach Ray Harford, who passed away on the morning of the opening day of the 2003/04 season at the age of 58.

NIGHT DREAM BELIEVER

There have been many instances of footballers dreaming about scoring in their next game the night before, and one Millwall player, Billy Hunter, was confident enough to relate his dream to a newspaper correspondent at breakfast on the morning of the FA Cup match at Sheffield Wednesday in February 1906. The young Scot revealed the details of his dream, by claiming that the result would be a draw of one goal each, and that he would score the Lions' goal.

Well, Billy's dream was fully realised that afternoon when from 30 yards he struck a goal for Millwall after 36 minutes. Wednesday duly equalised in the second half to level the scores, for the game to finish 1–1.

GO BAG A RABBIT

Many footballers like to face certain teams for various reasons. For some players it's because they always appear on the winning side, others like playing at particular grounds, while others seem to like facing a certain team because they always seem to score against them. Millwall's goal kings are no different.

Lions inside-forward Jimmy Constantine's own particular 'rabbit' were Ipswich Town. During the years 1949 to 1952, he scored in five consecutive games against the Tractor Boys. Jimmy had another club he liked to face, Walsall, having scored in four successive fixtures (between 1948 and 1951). Paul Ifill is another to obtain goals in five successive matches against Sheffield United between 2002 and 2004.

Other Lions to score in four games running against the same opponents are Alf Moule versus Aberdare Athletic (1924–26), and Jack Cock managed it against Preston North End (1928–31). Outside-left Jimmy Poxton was the thorn in local rivals Charlton Athletic's side from 1931 to 1933, while Stan Morgan was another of Walsall's tormentors from 1951 to 1953.

The late Keith Weller's fancy was Bolton Wanderers between 1967 and 1970, while his ex-Tottenham colleague Derek Possee found Luton Town to his liking from 1970 to 1973. Teddy Sheringham managed it against West Bromwich Albion and another United who Paul Ifill had in for was Colchester, with a quartet of goals between 1999 and 2001.

SUITS YOU, SIR

After manager Charlie Hewitt had changed Millwall's colours to royal blue shortly after his arrival in 1936, it forced the club to provide the match officials with grey alpaca blazers to avoid a colour clash for those who had arrived with blue or black ones.

When on their way to clinching the Division Two championship in 1969, Derby County arrived at The Den intending to play in an all-white strip, having not realised that Millwall had changed to a similar kit at the start of the 1968/69 season. The problem was solved when the Lions loaned County a set of red shirts and black shorts. It must have done the trick, for the Rams won 1–0. It was also the only occasion the legendary County captain Dave Mackay appeared in a Millwall shirt.

QUICK-FIRE SIGNING

In December 1947, when Millwall manager Jack Cock went to sign Coventry City centre-forward Norman Smith, a former fighter pilot in the Second World War, the Lions boss was in no mood for small talk. Arriving at Highfield Road at 2.20 p.m., he completed Norman's move in double quick time and left the ground by car at 2.39 p.m. to catch his train back to London. It was one of the quickest transfers on record.

SHOE SHINE BOY

The Millwall supporters adopted 'Shoe Shine Boy' as their signature tune during the Lions' epic FA Cup run of the 1936/37 season. The song, made famous by Bing Crosby (but according to one older supporter the original was from the UK's one and only Billy Cotton and his band), really took off when Millwall beat Fulham 2–0 in the third round.

It transpired that winger Reggie Smith used to sing the song in the dressing room and it caught on with the rest of the players, a point that had been confirmed by Millwall director Bill Nelan who also related that the manager Charlie Hewitt insisted the players shine their boots while singing it. The song retained its affection with fans during the following season when Millwall won promotion.

FAIR PLAY

In February 2002 Millwall put themselves in the frame for a FIFA Fair Play Award following a bizarre incident in the Avon Insurance Combination fixture against AFC Bournemouth at the New Den. Following a goalless first half, the second 45 minutes began when two Bournemouth players accidentally collided into one another.

After receiving treatment, the game restarted when Millwall's Mark Hicks played the ball towards the Bournemouth goal. However, the Cherries' goalkeeper Michael Menetrier was miles away and deep in thought as the ball entered the Bournemouth goal and he found himself unable to make a save. It was then that the fair play aspect was activated and the goalkeeper's blushes spared. Under clear instructions from Lions coach Joe McLaughlin, the Millwall players allowed the Bournemouth number 10, Amos Foyewa, a clear run on goal from the kick-off to make the score 1–1. Millwall's immediate reward for a magnanimous gesture saw them win the game 2–1 with a Ben May goal.

ASSISTING THE REF

When Millwall lost the second leg of a League Cup tie at Ipswich 0–5 in September 2000, the game came very close to being abandoned. The Lions were reduced to seven men through two sendings off and two injuries and having used all permitted substitutes, another Millwall player got injured. Despite the game being virtually over (Ipswich were leading 5–2 on aggregate), the referee Andy Hall – a zealot to the last – explained to the Millwall management that they must keep a seventh player on the field or the match would end. So it was left to the exhausted Tim Cahill to return to merely stand on the field of play for the last two minutes.

A BAD THROW

Following Canadian international Adrian Serioux's sending off in November 2004 for aiming his throw-in at Lee Cook of Queens Park Rangers, the laws were changed in 2005. Now, the opponent had to be at least 2 yards away from the thrower (instead of 1 yard) until the ball was in play. It became a cautionable offence in 2006 to stand any closer.

TUNNEL VISION

Bust-ups in the tunnel are not unusual at half time as Millwall and Sheffield United found to their cost at The Den in December 2004. Millwall skipper Kevin Muscat and Paddy Kenny the United goalkeeper were both given an early bath after coming to blows in the tunnel. Their actions were seen by the fourth official, and consequently both teams took to the field with ten men after the incident had been related to the managers.

MISCELLANEOUS SEASONAL RECORDS

Highest points total: 93, 2000/01
Most league wins: 30, 1927/28
Most home wins: 19, 1927/28
Most away wins: 12, 2008/09
Fewest defeats: 7, 1927/28, 1964/65
Fewest home defeats: 0, 1927/28, 1964/65, 1965/66, 1971/72 and 1984/85
Fewest away defeats: 6, 1926/27, 1937/38, 1952/53 and 1971/72
Lowest points total: 26, 1989/90
Fewest league wins: 5, 1989/90
Fewest home wins: 4, 1989/90
Fewest away wins: 1, 1989/90
Most defeats: 22, 1947/48, 1989/90, 2005/06 and 2007/08
Most home defeats: 11, 1957/58, 2005/06
Most away defeats: 19, 1955/56

Most league goals scored: 127, 1927/28
Most goals scored at home: 87, 1927/28
Most goals scored away: 41, 1960/61
Fewest goals conceded: 30, 1920/21
Fewest goals conceded at home: 8, 1920/21
Fewest goals conceded away: 22, 1920/21, 1937/38

Fewest league goals scored: 38, 1921/22
Fewest scored at home: 22, 1978/79
Fewest scored away: 12, 1986/87
Most goals conceded: 100, 1956/57
Most goals conceded at home: 36 1957/58
Most goals conceded away: 69, 1955/56

Most league draws: 18, 1921/22, 1922/23
Most home draws: 13, 1921/2
Most away draws: 10, 1969/70, 1971/72, 1975/76
Fewest draws: 4, 1949/50
Fewest home draws: 1, 1949/50
Fewest away draws: 1, 1946/47

DODGY SIGNINGS XI

Not every incoming transfer to Millwall sets the pulses racing and
for every good 'un signed, there will always be another who, for
one reason or another, fails to make an impact. The list below is
not necessarily the worst Millwall XI, but it may come close in
many supporters' selections.

1.   Lenny Pidgeley (2005)
2.   Gavin Maguire (1992)
3.   Phil Stamp (2001)
4.   Tony Kelly (1994)
5.   Sam Allardyce (1981)
6.   Dave Sinclair (1996)
7.   Jason Beckford (1994)
8.   Jason Dair (1996)
9.   Brian Dear (1969)
10.   Warren Patmore (1993)
11.   Lee Luscombe (1993)

SOUTHERN LEAGUE CENTENARY

In 1994 came the 100th anniversary of the Southern League's formation, in which Millwall Athletic played a leading part in bringing professional football to the south of England. The Lions, as part of the celebrations, were chosen to oppose a Southern Football League XI at Ashford Town FC in March 1994. Millwall, who twice won the championship title in its first two years, won the centenary game 2–1.

REVENGE IS SWEET

WHAT do you think of the Dark Blues now?
What do you think of the boys?
The Spurs thought them duffers,
But now it's them that suffers,
And they don't think them duffers now.

This is the *East End News* waxing lyrical after Millwall beat Tottenham Hotspur 3–0 at White Hart Lane on the opening day of the 1900/01 season, thus avenging the 3–1 defeat by Spurs at the East Ferry Road at the same stage in 1899.

A BLUE FOR THE 'WALL

The only player from either Oxford or Cambridge University to appear for Millwall is the Egyptian Hussein Hegazi (St Catharine's College, Cambridge). He appeared twice for the Lions in the Southern Alliance League in the 1912/13 season, against Croydon Common and Cardiff City, both of which ended in defeat.

He was, however, on the victorious side when he gained his football Blue for Cambridge when they defeated Oxford in

February 1914 at the Queen's Club – his light blue team winning 2–1. He later went on to represent Egypt in the 1920 and 1924 Olympic Games.

One other Oxbridge connection came nearly 90 years later when defender Graeme Paxton, who trialled at The Den in February 1998 but a failed medical examination, thus denying him a full-time contract, put the disappointment behind him by going up to Cambridge (St Edmund's) and won two Blues. The first in 2000 ended in a 1–0 defeat, but a 3–1 victory followed in 2001.

THE BUSBY BABES

On three occasions in 1953 Millwall met Manchester United at The Den, with the first coming on 10 January in a FA Cup third round tie which attracted a crowd of 35,652. It saw the Reds sneak a fortuitous 1–0 win through a late goal from Stan Pearson.

Having deprived Millwall of a replay in the FA Cup, United returned to The Den to play a friendly fixture on 2 May and an excellent gate of 14,127 fans witnessed an eight-goal bonanza – a 4–4 draw.

Manchester's recent signing from Barnsley, Tommy Taylor, scored what was regarded as the best goal of the game, when he ran half the length of the field, beating two defenders to place the ball into the corner of the net. United could have put the game beyond Millwall's reach had Roger Byrne scored from a penalty. Having failed to put some other decent chances away, the Reds were caught out when John Shepherd took advantage of Allenby Chilton's dithering to score a much-deserved equaliser.

The third encounter took place on 5 October and was to commemorate the inauguration of Millwall's new floodlights – and this was one game the Lions did win, 2–1. A crowd of 20,082 fans saw Millwall's Frank Neary at his belligerent best and Millwall gave a typical 'in-your-face' performance. Such was the intensity of the match that one scribe noted 'this was the most unfriendly friendly I can remember.'

Millwall took the lead on 10 minutes when Alex Jardine converted a penalty that was given for hand ball by Billy Foulkes. The lead was short-lived; Tommy Taylor headed home eight minutes later, but the Lions were in no mood to lose. Though they could not match United for skill and guile, they more than compensated for it with grit and determination.

The winner duly arrived in the 73rd minute when Alan Monkhouse curled over a corner. Neary, whose presence had unnerved the visitors' defence all night, challenged Ray Wood for the cross and resulted in the United goalkeeper finishing up in the net along the with ball and Monkhouse claiming the goal.

Sadly for Manchester United and ultimately England, the Busby Babes as they were coming to be known, were involved in the Munich Air Crash in February 1958. Two of the Reds who appeared at The Den, Roger Byrne and Tommy Taylor, lost their lives, while another two, Jackie Blanchflower and Peter Berry would never play again due to the injuries they sustained in the disaster. Both Ray Wood and Billy Foulkes survived the crash and carried on playing.

PLAY UP MILLWALL!

This poem was composed by John George Hames (1842–1917), probably in about 1909. He wrote many such pieces on a variety of subjects and was officially acknowledged by Queen Victoria for penning a poem in honour of her jubilee.

> There is trampling feet in the Subway
> As the eager crowd march through,
> To welcome the Boys in Blue.
> The surging, scampering, hurrying throng
> From Greenwich side to the Island,
> To a well-known spot are bound
> To the Britons' grand arena–
> To the Millwall Football Ground.

In the great Titanic struggle,
Where the 'Lions' dare and do
Millwall once more gives a welcome
To Millwall Boys in Blue,
Hark to the tempest of rolling sound!
Hark to the trumpet call!
It is the well-known battle cry:
Play up! Play up! Millwall!

We have all of us seen the 'Iron Horse'
And electric motors as well,
But we've an electric 'Hunter'
Tho' the proverb says 'Blood will tell'
Millwall has a Captain-General
A dashing and fearless back:
Often makes his opponents stare,
For Stevenson, foeman have great respect
He's a nut they find hard to crack.

The best managed club in the country,
So say London's daily press;
And one of the best of Chairmen
Is J.B. Skeggs, I guess.
George Saunders, Millwall's Team Manager,
His business he thoroughly knows,
And when 'Our Boys' have a big match on,
Well then – he don't care if it snows.

On Reserves Mr William Dickinson
Always keeps his paternal eye;
He has been with Club, since its early days,
In jolly good times gone by.
As Director, and also in finance,
M F C had Fred Thorne's chief care;
He can boast of the brilliant distinction
Of having been Poplar's Mayor.

The Directorate are men of the best
Men who are staunch and true:
Who have the Club's interest always at heart,
Who study the Boys in Blue.
Now, who has not heard of 'Tiny' Joyce,
The keeper of Millwall's goal?
As one of the best players
His name shines of fame's bright roll

There is Harvey Carmichael, the mighty,
His height is six-one-and-a-half;
And every time he defends our goal
The 'Islanders' have a good laugh.
Alf Twigg, Millwall's centre-forward
Often makes his opponents stare,
When he pops in a sudden 'dead homer.'
And they know all at once that he's there.

Jeffrey, Jones, Blythe and Elijah Moor,
Each one of them toes the line,
Real gems of the very first water,
As a star each was born to shine.
The best of luck of the Millwall team
Is the wish of us one and all,
Three ringing cheers for the Boys in Blue.
Play up, Play up, Millwall.

IS THIS SEAT TAKEN?

Although lifelong Millwall supporter Fred Swann had been deceased for five years his family were convinced he would like the idea of seeing his team at Wembley. So when the occasion arose in 1999, for the final of the Auto Windscreens Trophy versus Wigan Athletic, they purchased a ticket for Fred. Placing it on the vacant seat before the kick-off the family were sure that Fred was there in spirit, though watching from the grandstand in the sky he would have seen the Lions lose to a last-minute goal.

COULDN'T HIT A BARN DOOR ...

The list below contains a dozen of Millwall's lowest league top scorers, and these instances show the relegations far outweighing the promotions – 5 to 1.

Season	Player	Goals
1933/34 R	Laurie Fishlock	7
1947/48 R	Willie Hurrell	7
1974/75 R	Brian Clark	7
2007/08	Gary Alexander	7
1921/22	Billy Keen	8
1975/76 P	Phil Summerill/Gordon Hill	8
1980/81	Nick Chatterton	8
1922/23	Alf Moule	9
1978/79	Ian Pearson	9
1978/79 R	John Seasman	9
1989/90 R	Tony Cascarino/Teddy Sheringham	9
2003/04	Tim Cahill/Neil Harris	9

R = Relegated   P = Promoted

GROUND CLOSURES

Crowd trouble has been a monkey on Millwall's back practically since their formation, and it has necessitated The Den at Cold Blow Lane being closed on five separate occasions. The first, for two weeks, occurred from 22 November until 4 December 1920. It followed disturbances during the match with Newport County in October when a nasty, nay brutal, County side were beaten 1–0. Their tactics and overall display had wound the crowd up, and they began bombarding the County goalkeeper, Jackie Cooper, with various missiles.

One contemporary assessment described Cooper as being 'as mad as a hatter' – apparently he took matters into his own hands, leaping over the surrounding fence to confront some of the miscreants, only to be flattened by a right hook and then unceremoniously manhandled back on to the pitch.

The ground closure was to hit Millwall financially, but after arranging with Norwich City to reverse the home and away fixtures (teams then, used to play each other on following Saturdays), the change was surprisingly, albeit reluctantly, granted by the Football League. This was how they got around the closure.

A combination of poor results, some indifferent refereeing and a large dose of misfortune were the cause of Millwall suffering their first relegation in 1934. It was following Bradford's 1–0 victory in March that year and the reaction by some of the fans who targeted the field of play with a selection of missiles (including oranges), which resulted in The Den being closed for a second time.

In what was another unsuccessful fight against the drop, Millwall again incurred the wrath of the FA. In what had been described as a 'rip-roaring match' against Barnsley in October 1947 (with the Lions leading 3–2), the match official awarded Barnsley a late penalty, from which they equalised. Cue pandemonium. Spectators encroached onto the pitch to confront the referee, but thankfully they were stopped before reaching him. The referee became the target of the missile-hurlers, and when he left the ground, he foolishly identified himself to fan who then tried to assault him.

For this latest misdemeanour Millwall were fined £100 and the ground was closed for seven days. It forced the Lions to play their 'home' fixture versus Newcastle United at Selhurst Park, the home of Crystal Palace.

The next spell of trouble came just over two years later (in January 1950) in another home defeat, this time by Exeter City. Exeter won the match, a very contentious FA Cup first round tie, 5–3. The game, in which three of City's goals had been hotly disputed, resulted in Millwall finishing with nine men. Following the game, a gang numbering between 150 and 200 ambushed the referee and his two linesmen. The controversy surrounding this game raged and even manager Charlie Hewitt was forced to air his views in the following week's match programme. Once again The Den was closed for a week with another £100 fine finding its way into the FA coffers. Ironically the game the Lions would have to rearrange was against Newport County of all teams. Instead of playing the Welsh side on 4 February in the league game, they arranged a friendly match with them at Newport, who won 7–1.

The fifth closure and hopefully the last in this sorry saga came following Ipswich Town's 6–1 success in the sixth round FA Cup match in March 1978. The violence that day had exceeded anything that gone before at The Den. Closing the ground for 14 days meant Millwall, who again were facing relegation, were left in a quandary in locating a club or clubs willing to accommodate them for staging their fixtures against Mansfield Town and Bristol Rovers.

Portsmouth's Fratton Park became the venue for the game against Rovers, and with Millwall needing every point they could get, a 1–3 defeat was not what the doctor ordered. It was another south coast club, Brighton & Hove Albion, who offered their Goldstone Ground for the Mansfield game. Vehement protests from the residents and councillors of Hove saw the Albion later withdraw the offer, though. Eventually the banning period had passed and it left the authorities no other option but to let Millwall play the Mansfield game at The Den.

One last thought which illustrates the mindset of a section of the Millwall support, came during the 1952/53 season when manager Charlie Hewitt received an anonymous letter the Friday before a game which threatened:

'Drop —, or we shall see the ground is closed'

The author of this piece of nonsense claimed to be a supporter of 30 years' standing (some supporter), and said he had prevented a section of the crowd from throwing missiles at the player in question the previous week. Hewitt said, 'This particular player is one of my best. In any case I should never take notice of such a threat.' He also added, 'I did not think it necessary to bring in the police. It is a job I can handle myself.'

WHO'S BEEN A NAUGHTY BOY THEN?

Thankfully, and as far as we know, there has not been any Millwall player charged with match-fixing allegations or any form of corruption that might have influenced the outcome of a game.

But the Lions have had players who have fallen foul of the authorities while with other clubs. In January 1907 Millwall welcomed back Sammy 'Snowball' Frost, who had been suspended for six months when his former club Manchester City had been involved in illegal payments to their players.

Accompanying Sam to North Greenwich was former England goalkeeper Jack Hillman who, like Frost, had also been banned for a similar period. He was no stranger to the more unsavoury aspects of the game and indeed while he was at Burnley he was suspended for a year after he attempted to bribe a Nottingham Forest player. Jack's claim that he was only joking did not wash with the FA, who banned him. It turned into an expensive joke, for not only did he lose a year's wages but also a £300 benefit.

Jack's Millwall career lasted for just two games: on his debut he kept a clean sheet in the 7–0 demolition of Queens Park Rangers, but week later in the FA Cup at Bristol Rovers, he damaged a shoulder in attempting save Rovers' second goal. So severe was the injury that Jack was forced to retire from the game completely.

Millwall's third player to be involved in a fraud conspiracy was Arthur Whalley who played just nine times for the Lions after joining them from Charlton Athletic in October 1924. His misdemeanour was his involvement in football's first betting scandal that centred on the Good Friday 1915 encounter between Manchester United and Liverpool at Old Trafford. United needed to win to avoid relegation, a feat which they accomplished by two goals to nil. The fans became suspicious though, as did the referee, and along with the continued rumours it would lead to certain players being incriminated.

The outcome of the tribunal in December 1915 saw Arthur and two United colleagues, Sandy Turnbull and Enoch West, plus four Liverpool players all receiving life bans from the FA. All barring West, the other participants' punishment was lifted in 1919. When Arthur retired from football, he appropriately went to work for a bookmaker in Manchester.

HE SAID WHAT?

'This is worse than a whole season of cup ties.'

The above is the last line of Private John Borthwick's letter to his manager at Millwall, Bert Lipsham, that described his experiences around Delville Wood in July 1916, during the First World War.

'Anyone who thinks Millwall won't stay up at the top is wrong.'

Dave Beasant, the Newcastle United goalkeeper, after letting in four goals at The Den in November 1988.

When television presenter Jim Rosenthal asked: 'So what's an American doing playing in goal for Millwall?' Lion Kasey Keller replied: 'I'm trying to keep the ball out.'

'Dance? Dance? I'll dance on your f****** head if you don't f*** off.'

Terry Hurlock, Millwall's powerhouse midfielder in answer to a misguided Icelander who requested a turn around the dancefloor.

This took place when some off-duty members on the England B summer tour of Iceland in 1989 had inadvertently wandered into Reykjavik nightclub that was frequented by some rather nice young men.

'It was a tremendous atmosphere and a magnificent crowd, who were very hostile. They even booed us off the coach as we arrived, which is a first for us.'

Rotherham United manager Ronnie Moore's post-match comment after his team had been beaten 4–0 in a top-of-the-table clash at The Den in April 2001.

'I played with Ron in about 100 reserve games and according to Ron he was man of the match in at least 99 of them.'

So said former Millwall skipper Dennis Jackson about Ron Atkinson, later to become Manchester United's manager. The two had been team-mates at Aston Villa in the late 1950s.

A ROUND DOZEN

Over a period of six seasons (1906–12) when both Millwall and Leyton were members of the Southern League, they opposed one another in a dozen games. Nothing odd in that you might say, but curiously the twelve fixtures were equally divided into six victories each.

Another anomaly in this unique set is that both clubs achieved their best wins at each other's grounds, with Millwall gaining a 4–1 victory in September 1907, in which Alf Twigg scored a hat-trick. Leyton obtained their best result, a 3–0 success, in December 1910.

The full list is:

	Home	Away
1906/07	2–0	2–3
1907/08	1–0	4–1
1908/09	3–1	1–2
1909/10	0–2	3–2
1910/11	0–3	1–2
1911/12	2–1	0–1

CALLED TO THE BAR

Football has not always been flushed with money, especially down in the lower echelons, and players have had to seek employment outside the game to make ends meet. One popular route has been the licensed trade in a pub normally in the vicinity of their former ground, where they could welcome supporters before or after the match.

One of Millwall's well-known players to enter the trade was former skipper Len Graham who managed pubs in London's West End and Bethnal Green before and during the Second World War. Following hostilities he became a landlord in Chelsea when it was announced that he was taking over the running of the Beehive.

Len's team-mate from the great 1928 Millwall side and former Lions manager Jack Cock also became a publican after he left The Den when he acquired the White Hart in New Cross Road. The iconic Barry Kitchener became the guv'nor for a while of the Shard Arms along the Old Kent Road.

Following his retirement from the game through injury, full-back Brian Brown later became the tenant of the Magnet and Dewdrop on the Isle of Dogs in the mid-1970s. The licensee of The Vulcan, another watering hole on the island, was Brian's team-mate Dave Donaldson. While another defender, centre-half Ray Brady, took over the New Jolly Caulkers that was located on Lower Road, opposite one of the entrances of the long-gone Surrey Commercial Docks, before taking over the Railway and Bicycle in Sevenoaks where remained for over 25 years.

A team-mate of both Graham and Cock was Southampton-born Alan Noble who became host at the Pier View at Cowes on the Isle of Wight, while a latter-day Lion, goalkeeper Chris Day and his wife became the owners of the Crooked Billet at Stevenage in 2008. When former captain General Stevenson retired in September 1910 he returned to his native Lancashire to take over a public house at Padiham, near Burnley.

Bob Hill, who had a season with Millwall in 1898/99, had originally bought himself out of the Army for £40 to play professionally and later became a publican in his native Forfar in 1901. His son Frank was later to become manager of Charlton Athletic in November 1961. Hill's team-mate and fellow Scot Bob Tannahill was later 'called to the bar' in Bolton in 1911.

SPOT-KICK MANIA(C)

Millwall's youth team had cause to remember referee Mr Biddulph, who presided over two of their matches in the first half of the 1993/94 season. He awarded no fewer than six penalties against the Lions youngsters. His first treble came when he gave Charlton Athletic three spot-kicks on 25 September in a match Millwall eventually won 6–3.

But lightning was to strike for the second time seven weeks later when Arsenal were the opponents in the South East Counties League. It saw the official award the Gunners three penalties from which they duly converted to win 3–0. To rub salt into the wound, Lion cub Kevin Hatcher was also sent off in the match.

ACROSS THE POND

Sending players to North America from these shores has been an ongoing practice since the game became professional and listed below are some former Millwall personnel who found benefit by plying their trade on the other side of the pond.

Sam Allardyce	Tampa Bay Rowdies 1983
Peter Anderson	San Diego Sockers 1978; Tampa Bay Rowdies 1978, 1980
Tommy Baldwin	Seattle Sounders 1975
Les Barrett	California Surf 1978, 1979
Graham Brown	Portland Timbers 1975, 1977
Dennis Burnett	St Louis Stars 1975, 1977

Sandy Caie	Westmount; Sons of Canada; Rosedale (Montreal) all before 1914
Danny Dichio	Toronto FC 2007
Mike Dillon	Montreal Olympics 1972; New York Cosmos 1975, 1977; Washington Diplomats 1978, 1979
Willie Donnachie	Portland Timbers 1980
Ray Evans	St Louis Stars 1977; California Surf 1978; Seattle Sounders 1982, 1983
George Graham	California Surf 1978
Steve Harrison	Vancouver Whitecaps 1978
Joe Haverty	Chicago Sting 1967; Kansas City Spurs 1968
Austin Hayes	Los Angeles Aztecs 1978
Gordon Hill	Chicago Sting 1975; Montreal Manic 1981; Chicago Sting 1982; New York Arrows 1983; Kansas City Comets 1983; Tacoma Stars 1984
Darren Huckerby	San Jose Earthquakes 2008
John Jackson	St Louis Stars 1977; California Surf 1978
Gordon Jago	Tampa Bay Rowdies 1978 to 1982
Nicky Johns	Tampa Bay Rowdies 1978
Len Julians	Detroit Cougars 1968
Tony Kinsella	Tampa Bay Rowdies 1981
Barry Kitchener	Tampa Bay Rowdies 1979
Steve Lovell	Memphis Rogues 1979
Chris McGrath	Tulsa Roughnecks 1981, 1982
Dave Mehmet	Tampa Bay Rowdies 1981
Dean Neal	Tulsa Roughnecks 1981
Jimmy Nicholl	Toronto Blizzard 1984
Graham Paddon	Tampa Bay Rowdies 1978
Derek Possee	Vancouver Whitecaps 1977, 1979
Bruce Rioch	Seattle Sounders 1980, 1981
Bill Ritchie	Montreal Scottish, New Bedford Whalers both 1926; Boston Wonder Workers 1928
Barry Rowan	Oakland Clippers 1967; Detroit Cougars 1968; Dallas Tornados 1971; Toronto Metros 1972

Barry Salvage	St Louis Stars 1977
Adrian Serioux	Metro Stars/Red Bull New York 2006; Houston Dynamo Toronto FC Dallas all in 2006
Steve Sherwood	Hartford Bicentennials 1976
Derek Smethurst	Tampa Bay Rowdies 1975, 1978; San Diego 1978; Seattle Sounders 1979, 1980
Bryan Snowdon	Detroit Cougars 1968
Jim Standen	Detroit Cougars 1968
Alex Stepney	Dallas Tornados 1979, 1980
David Stride	Memphis Rogues 1979, 1980; Minnesota Kicks 1981; Jacksonville 1982
Jim Terris	New York Field Club 1923; Indiana Flooring 1924; New York Giants 1927
Keith Weller	New England Teamen 1978, 1980; Fort Lauderdale Strikers 1980, 1983; Tacoma Stars 1984
Alan West	Minnesota Kicks 1976, 1979

IT'S MILLWALL FROM THE PAVILION END

Although ground-sharing between big city clubs might be the norm in certain countries in continental Europe, the notion of it happening in the United Kingdom has always had a lukewarm reception at best. However, one form of sharing that had once been commonplace was the accommodation of both cricket and football utilising the same venue.

The last occurrence of Millwall appearing at a cricketing arena was on 13 April 1971 when they lost to Sheffield United at Bramall Lane, then also the headquarters of Yorkshire County Cricket Club. The last cricket fixture held at this venue was on 7 August 1973. Nearer home and in their formative years, Millwall played a number of times at the County Ground, Leyton, the home of Essex CCC, before their relocation to Chelmsford. One of Millwall's heaviest defeats came here in January 1893 when they were beaten 10–1 by Old Carthusians in the London Charity Cup.

Another London venue, which is the second oldest Test ground in the world, is the Kennington Oval and it was here, a week after the Leyton débâcle that Millwall suffered a second horrendous cup exit in the London Senior. This time it was at the hands of Old Westminsters who won 6–0, and in this game came Millwall's first use of a permitted substitute, when Arthur Burton replaced Tom Horne who had broken a leg.

The trend continued after Millwall Athletic became founder members of the Southern League in 1894 and some of their opening encounters with Southampton St Mary's took place on grounds where Hampshire CCC also played – the Antelope and the County Ground. Along the coast in Sussex Millwall have made appearances at the County Ground, Hove, when entertained by Brighton United in the 1898/99 season and in two visits there Millwall managed only a loss and a draw. The other Sussex ground to host Millwall was the Saffrons at Eastbourne, where Millwall took on the local club in four friendly matches between November 1894 and March 1898.

The Lions have played at the County Ground at Northampton where the football team nicknamed the Cobblers shared with the county cricket club for nearly a century and was probably the one venue where Millwall had a decent playing record. Lastly, it's back to Yorkshire, and the Park Avenue ground in Bradford. Millwall's initial visit there resulted in a 1–0 victory in Bradford's first season as professional club, after they became, surprisingly, members of the Southern League. Sadly, neither first-class cricket nor football is played at Park Avenue now.

CHAIRMAN OF THE BOARD

Stability at the top of a football club is vital and in Millwall's long and varied history this has largely appeared to be the case. Up until 1948 only four men had held the lofty position of chairman since the club was formed in 1885. The upheaval following Theo Paphitis' resignation in 2005 and relegation a year later, however, witnessed a very large dose of instability.

The Lions had no less than four incumbent chairmen in a little over six months in a turbulent 2005, and it was not until the arrival of the American investor John Berylson in 2007 that the good ship Millwall finally sailed into calmer waters.

The full list is:

Dr J Murray Leslie	1885–93
Colin Gordon	1893–1902
James Skeggs	1902–15
Tom Thorne	1915–48
Percy Higson	1948
Dr David Eppel	1948–51
Capt Norman Weedon	1951–6
F.C. 'Mickey' Purser	1956–74
Herbert Burnige	1974–8
Len Eppel	1978–81
Alan Thorne	1981–6
Reg Burr	1986–96
Peter Mead	1995–7
Theo Paphitis	1997–2005
Jeff Burnige	2005
Peter de Savary	2005–6
Stewart Till	2006–7
John Berylson	2007–

THE ANGLO-ITALIAN CUP

This competition is a bit of a misnomer as far as Millwall are concerned, the Lions having played just four matches in the tournament, with not one Italian opponent to be seen anywhere.

The clubs the Lions faced in 1992/93 and 1993/94 were Charlton Athletic (twice), Crystal Palace and a trip to Portsmouth, which is about the nearest Millwall got to Italy.

HENRY 'ARRY BOY' CRIPPS

Always known to the fans at The Den as 'Arry Boy', Cripps was a free transfer signing from West Ham United in 1961 and would over the next 13 years become a firm favourite down Cold Blow Lane with a never-say-die attitude that was matched by his insatiable enthusiasm and love of football.

Even so, it did not stop various managers from trying to replace him. Harry, however, would see off all the pretenders for his coveted place. Of course he had his bad days, and he even got booed on occasions, but he never hid or shirked his responsibilities. And like a fine wine, Harry matured with age and his ten goals from full-back in 1970/71 showed how much he had improved as a footballer to become a valuable member of the team.

Stories about him are legendary but one tale arose when renowned journalist and broadcaster Bryon Butler described Harry back in the mid-1960s as 'an archetypal Third Division full-back, part Neanderthal, part desperado, part prison warder.' Shortly afterwards, however, whispers began reaching Bryon – ''Arry wants a word with you,' ''Arry Boy is asking after your health' and 'watch out for 'Arry.' There was even a postcard: 'Mr Cripps will be in touch. Soon.'

After Butler's appraisal of Harry, the two finally met during one close-season when Butler was relaxing in the pavilion at a cricket ground in Kent. A heavy hand landed on his shoulder: 'Gotcha!' it was 'Arry, looming very large. ''Ave a big drink,' he said. 'Nobody's called me an archetype before.'

He may not have been the greatest player seen in Millwall colours, but to many Lions fans he was the typical Millwall player and more often than not he would appear in a lot of supporters' all-time greatest Millwall team. The world became a less happy place following Harry's passing at the age of 54 in December 1995. He was a true Lions legend.

A little ditty some of the fans would sing from behind the Cold Blow Lane goal went like this:

> Harry, Harry break us a leg,
> Break us a leg,
> Break us a leg,
>
> Harry, Harry break us a leg,
> A yard above the knee.

THE BEGGING BOWL

Millwall as a club are now on a fairly stable financial footing, but this has not always been the case. Since the Second World War there have been various fundraising enterprises aimed at the hardcore support. There was the 'Million Penny Fund' in the 1950s and a decade or so later Millwall Pools Ltd was formed to raise revenue. Part of the remit was to arrange a match for The Den Rebuilding Fund that took place in April 1968 when Millwall faced an Internationals Club team, which included former Lion Pat Saward, the ex-England skipper Billy Wright and future England manager Bobby Robson.

To boost the coffers the Lions themselves engaged the services of two football fanatics from the world of showbusiness. Comedian Jimmy Tarbuck and singer and Millwall fan Des O'Connor were to be Millwall's new strike force for the evening. A crowd of 4,600 saw the Lions achieve a 3–2 victory, with Des snatching a late winner after being set up by Keith Weller. The 'begging bowl', aka the rebuilding fund, benefitted to the sum of £750. Not one member of the Internationals XI claimed their expenses.

THE MODEL LION

When The Den was officially opened on 22 October 1910, Millwall were presented with a model lion by Mr J. Jarrett jnr, on which was an inscription in Scots-Gaelic which read:

Ar Cul Ri Naimh Cha Churi Gu Brach

The translation of this purported to be: 'We Fear No Foe Where E'er We Go'. However, it transpired later that the motto was meant to have read 'We Will Never Turn Our Backs To The Enemy'.

One would assume the Scottish version of Gaelic has not changed all that much over the last 100 years or so, but further research has shown the modern translation does not appear to apply to either of the above.

Below are hopefully the correct translations:

We Fear No Foe Where E'er We Go
Chan Eagal Dhuinn Ge B' E Caite'n Teid Sinn

We Will Never Turn Our Backs To The Enemy
Cha Chuir Sinn Ar Cul Ris An Namhaid A-Chaoidh

ONE-GAME WONDERS

Up to 90 players have made just one appearance for Millwall in bona fide first-team games since they became a professional entity. Many have made their sole outing as a substitute. But the following five have all managed to score a goal in their only match:

E. Jones*   versus Royal Ordnance, 10 November 1894, Southern League
E. Coggins   versus West Ham United, 29 February 1904, London League

D. Ridley   versus Northampton Town, 5 January 1946,
                 FA Cup
R. Phillips   versus Northampton Town, 7 January 1946,
                 FA Cup
A. Sunnocks   versus Charlton Athletic, 25 March 1957,
                 Kent FA Cup Final

* Eddie 'Taff' Jones had scored goals for Millwall in the early cup
ties when the club was an amateur organisation. The above game
was his only match as a professional before he reverted back to his
previous status.

MILLWALL ALLITERATIVES

A team comprised of former Millwall players with the same first
and second initials:

Lawrie
Leslie

| Brian | Colin | Alan | Sean |
| Brown | Cooper | Anderson | Sparham |

| Freddie | Dave | John | Chris |
| Fisher | Donaldson | Jones | Clarke |

Alf   Jimmy
Ackerman   Jinks

RIGHT SHIRT, WRONG BADGE

Prior to the opening of the 1967/68 season Millwall's striking
new royal blue shirts arrived and after the parcels were hurriedly
opened it was discovered the suppliers had placed a Fulham badge
on the shirts by mistake. How the Lions roared.

LIFESAVERS

In the summer of 1993 former Millwall midfielder George Jacks was on holiday in Crete and made himself a hero when the local press reported the story of him saving the life of a 6ft plus 18-year-old youth who had got into difficulties while swimming in the sea. No mean feat this, given George's stature of 5ft 6in tall and around 11 stone in weight!

George is not the only Lion to risk his own personal safety: a similar occurrence happened to centre-half Archie Gomm who received an award from the Royal Humane Society after he had saved a young boy from drowning at Hornsea, Yorkshire, in July 1926.

FREDDIE FOX

There cannot be too many players who have appeared for their country before making their club debut. Well, this was the case for goalkeeper Freddie Fox, who won his only cap for England in a game against France in Paris on 21 May 1925, so becoming the second Millwall goalkeeper to play for England. Fred's selection was to become a bone of contention among some Gillingham historians, who wrongly assumed that he was their player when the game was played.

However, Fred had been a Millwall player for the best part of three weeks by the time Millwall faced Gillingham at The Den in the last match of the 1924/25 season on 2 May 1925. Although he had become an England prospect while with Gillingham, the bottom line is that he was a definitely a Lion when Paris beckoned in the spring of 1925.

Fred's first and only England start was not all plain sailing; indeed in a low-key first 45 minutes he had not touched the ball once. But the match ignited in the second half as England raced into a three-goal lead. But with 15 minutes left Fred was forced from the field of play when he sustained a kick in the face. England, already down to ten men, subsequently held on to win 3–2 with nine fit players.

At the end of the following August, Fred finally made his first-team bow between the sticks at Crystal Palace where Millwall gained a 2–1 victory.

AN EXPENSIVE PAIR OF SHORTS

This escapade arose when Millwall entertained Cambridge University in a friendly fixture at the East Ferry Road in November 1903. One of the light blues' participants was A.F. Leach-Lewis, who prided himself on being well prepared for a game by bringing extra pairs of boot laces, plasters and bandages.

On this particular occasion, however, the normally thorough student had forgotten to pack a pair of shorts. His blushes were momentarily spared when a Millwall attendant appeared with a selection of shorts of various sizes. After trying around twenty pairs, A.F. finally chose a pair made of white calico.

These seemed utterly inappropriate for such a burly defender of 6ft-plus and tipping the scales at around 15 stone. So tight-fitting were the shorts that he was feeling very self-conscious, but this was not his only concern of the afternoon. Lining up for Millwall that day was none other than our old friend George Robey, who was sure to make fun of the student's predicament.

Having endured the 90 minutes of football, any thoughts Leach-Lewis had of putting the episode behind him were jolted when he received a letter from the player whose shorts he had borrowed, saying, 'last Saturday you borrowed my shorts, will you please return them?'

Leach-Lewis' riposte was that he left them with the attendant, plus a little money for them to be laundered. A response by the Lion was that the official had no recollection of the return of the shorts. This left the Cambridge man no other option than to offer to pay for some replacement shorts, which the dutiful Lion complied with and then forwarded him the receipt.

The undergraduate, thinking that a new pair would set him back no more than 1s 11d, was flabbergasted when the bill arrived displaying the princely sum of 10s 6d for a pair of 'Best Serge Shorts' or 'knickers' as they were then called.

It appeared Leach-Lewis' brief visit to the Isle of Dogs appeared to be not only embarrassing but very expensive. Being stitched up by the Millwall player (identity unknown) is one thing, but to suffer the Millwall official's (also anonymous) bout of amnesia must have been a tad galling. Many years later Allen Francis Leach-Lewis bumped into George Robey at a cricket match where they reminisced over many things, including that expensive pair of shorts.

BRING ON THE SCOTS

The Lions' early connection with Scotland is well known and matches against clubs from north of the border became a regular occurrence, especially after Millwall took the decision to become a professional club. The full list of the games is:

Battlefield	H	3–1	23/3/1894
Clyde	H	6–2	15/9/1894
Renton	H	1–2	22/9/1894
Kilmarnock	H	2–0	31/12/1894
Battlefield	H	0–1	12/4/1895
Third Lanark	H	0–1	13/4/1895
Battlefield	H	3–0	3/4/1896
Dundee	H	0–1	7/4/1896
St Bernard's	H	0–0	26/10/1896
Battlefield	H	4–0	16/4/1897
Rangers	H	1–0	17/4/1897
Scottish Amateurs	H	5–0	8/4/1898
Renton	H	7–0	3/9/1898
Scottish Amateurs	H	2–0	31/3/1899
Rangers	H	5–1	1/4/1899
Glasgow University	H	3–0	26/12/1899

Scottish Amateurs	H	1–0	13/4/1900
Scottish Amateurs	H	5–1	5/4/1901
Third Lanark	H	1–0	11/4/1903
Celtic	H	1–1	2/9/1903
Celtic	H	3–2	25/4/1949
Dundee United	H	2–1	12/5/1951
Raith Rovers	H	3–3	3/5/1952
Raith Rovers	H	2–3	20/4/1953
Dundee	H	3–0	25/10/1954
Raith Rovers	H	3–3	13/4/1959
Queen of the South	A	1–3	21/3/1960
Dundee United	H	0–2	17/4/1961
Dundee	A	0–3	2/8/1967
Falkirk	A	5–2	5/8/1967
Dundee	H	8–0	5/8/1968
Raith Rovers	H	4–1	26/7/1969
Raith Rovers	A	2–1	2/8/1969
Dundee United	H	2–1	4/8/1969
Dundee	H	5–0	1/8/1970
Motherwell	H	1–0	12/2/1971
Hibernian	H	1–1	17/8/1990
Ayr United	A	3–4	27/7/1996
Stranraer	A	4–1	31/7/1996
Kilmarnock	A	2–4	3/8/1996
Heart of Midlothian	N	1–1	17/7/2004*
Dundee	A	1–2	14/7/2007
Falkirk	A	0–1	18/7/2007
Motherwell	A	1–1	21/7/2007
Heart of Midlothian	H	2–3	31/7/2010

* played in Canada

THE 'B' TEAM

When Millwall commenced the 1960/61 season at York City contained in their line-up were six players whose surnames began with the letter 'B', they were: Pat and Ray Brady, Dave Bumstead, Ray Brand, Peter Burridge and Joe Braodfoot.

The same six appeared in the next match, but the sequence did not occur again until the home match against Wrexham in March 1961 when the Bradys, Bumstead, Burridge and Broadfoot were joined by Brian Bevan, who was making his third and last appearance for the Lions.

ENGLAND EXPECTS

Millwall has been the launch-pad the for some outstanding players since the Second World War who have gone to play for England, with three of them starting their professional careers at The Den. Those seven are listed with their first England appearance:

1.	Alex Stepney	v	Sweden	1968	3–1
2.	Keith Weller	v	Wales	1974	2–0
3.	Gordon Hill	v	Italy	1976	3–2
4.	John Fashanu	v	Chile	1989	0–0
5.	Teddy Sheringham	v	Poland	1993	1–1
6.	Neil Ruddock	v	Nigeria	1995	1–0
7.	Colin Cooper	v	Sweden	1995	3–3

A MYTH PERPETUATED

The old adage of 'don't let the truth get in the way of a good story' has been applied to many published articles over the years and here's one concerning a footballer named Frank Barson who had played for Aston Villa, Manchester United and England who was alleged to have appeared in a game at Millwall.

The story supposedly surfaced in a book by a well-known former England player and was then brought again into the public domain when another publication hit the bookshops in 2008 about the game's greatest characters, in which Barson was featured. Barson was a rough, tough and uncompromising centre-half whose disciplinary record of sendings-off and other misdemeanours was as long as your arm. Why The Den was chosen for the perpetuation of the myth can only be imagined. But the passage from the book read:

> In a match at Millwall he [Barson] became involved in a series of personal feuds and just before half time he was injured in a clash of heads. Covered in mud and blood he staggered to the dressing room for treatment, booed every step of the way by The Den fans. During the break he changed his strip and had a bandage wrapped around his head to protect the wound. As he emerged for the second half, a Millwall supporter yelled 'The disguise hasn't worked Barson, we can still recognise yer.'

A great yarn indeed, but sadly untrue, for research has revealed that Barson never played at The Den and when the compiler of book was contacted, he offered no confirmation but claimed it was a good story and one too good not to publish.

A TALE FROM THE RIVER (DANUBE) BANK

Another episode in Millwall's colourful history occurred in December 1953 and following a lot of secretive meetings it was announced Millwall would be signing a Hungarian footballer. A scoop indeed, especially after Hungary had become the first foreign side to inflict upon England their first defeat on home soil a month earlier.

The gentleman concerned was Janos Kedves, aged 26 who, had it not been for his political views, might have been a member of the victorious Hungarian team at Wembley. Kedves had been in England for something like five years and had spent time up in Lancashire before two weeks of cloak-and-dagger shenanigans took place and Janos or 'Johnny' as he was later called, was offered a player-coach deal just before Christmas.

It was a friend of Millwall manager Charles Hewitt who informed him about Kedves and following ten days of enquiries and plenty of legwork, Hewitt was confident enough to inform his chairman Captain Norman Weedon and a couple of other directors. By keeping the transaction on a 'need to know' basis, the quartet agreed to keep the deal under wraps until it was successfully concluded.

A bubbly Hewitt was excited to state, 'I was sufficiently impressed by what he obviously knew about the game to sign him.' Kedves had apparently learnt his football skill with the legendary Hungarian skipper Ferenc Puskás and if this was the case, then the Lions would have pulled-off an intriguing coup.

A five-year exile from top-class football would have certainly hampered Kedves' fitness, but whatever class he had would have remained. Sadly though, Hewitt's assessment after all these considerations of having gained a player worth £30,000 for a £10 signing-on fee would ring hollow. Just a month into the New Year Kedves had departed Cold Blow Lane for good, having impressed no one at the club, least of all the players.

A SAD FAREWELL

Hugh Morris was a very experienced Welsh international who signed for Millwall Athletic in May 1897. Here he would link once again with fellow countryman Joe Davies, whom Morris had played alongside at Manchester City and Sheffield United. The pair were also born in the same town of Chirk.

When the rest of his new Millwall team-mates, including Joe, were preparing to face Chatham at home on 20 September, poor Hugh was succumbing to the dreaded disease tuberculosis at his home in North Wales. At the young age of 25 he had not kicked a ball in anger for his new club.

MILLWALL'S WELSH DRAGONS

This formidable-looking team from the valleys whose contribution to Millwall's history should not be forgotten, contains eight Welsh internationals, two of whom were tragically killed in the First World War:

1.	Fred Griffiths	(1900–1)
2.	John Evans	(1946–50)
3.	Dennis John	(1962–6)
4.	Steve Lovell	(1982–7)
5.	Brian Law	(1997–9)
6.	Ernie Watkins	(1901–6)
7.	Steve Lowndes	(1983–6)
8.	Johnny Williams	(1913–15)
9.	Wally Davis	(1911–15)
10.	John Lyons	(1979–81)
11.	Dick Jones	(1899–1901 & 1902–10)

Manager: Kenny Jackett (2007–)

BIG BROTHER

Following their decision to become a professional organisation in 1893, Millwall like many other clubs, looked to Scotland to enhance their playing staff and persuaded two Scots, Alexander McKenzie and Hugh Robertson to throw in their lot with the Dockers in the metropolis.

However, a while after engaging the pair the Millwall executive received a most unwelcome surprise in the shape of a demand of £100 from Everton, on the grounds that they held the Football League registration of the two Scots. How they claimed this is not certain, but one thing was: that neither Robertson nor McKenzie had even been south of the border before.

Millwall rightly refused to play ball and admitted no liability. But the other Football League clubs backed Everton and promptly applied a boycott by cancelling already arranged friendly games at Millwall. This left them with a very distressed-looking fixture list. Despite Everton's big brother approach, a compromise was reached when Millwall agreed to pay them £25. In the end it would appear money well spent as both Alex and Hugh played leading roles in helping Millwall Athletic win the first Southern League title in 1895.

MILLWALL'S OLYMPIANS

With the Olympic Games taking place in London in 2012, a Millwall link to the sporting jamboree would be a welcome addition to those which already exist. The very first Olympian to appear in Lions colours was Joe Dines, who assisted Millwall during the First World War and became a gold medallist when Great Britain won the Olympic football title in 1912.

Around that same time the Lions had played Hussein Hegazi in a couple of games before he returned to Egypt and he went on to appear in the games of 1920 and 1924 in the dual role of player and coach. Three former Lions would also appear in the Olympics as trainers – two of them Scottish. Billy Maxwell who had two seasons at North Greenwich led Belgium in the first two games held after the First World War, in Antwerp and Paris.

The other Scot was Billy Hunter who became the first player Millwall received a transfer fee for when he joined Bolton Wanderers in 1909. He became the coach of Turkey and his first match came against Czechoslovakia at the 1924 Olympiad. Millwall born and bred, Billy 'Banger' Voisey was part of the Great Britain coaching set-up for the Berlin games in 1936.

After a lull of 60 years, and an alteration to the rules in relation to the status of players appearing in the Olympics, Millwall benefitted from the changes made. American goalkeeper Kasey Keller participated at the 1996 Atlanta tournament for the USA and another to appear for the host nation in 2000 was the 22-year-old Australian Lucas Neill.

THE PRODIGAL SONS

The Bible tells us of the prodigal son, but Millwall have had many
in their history – players who have come back for a second spell
and here is a selection:

John Brearley	Joe Broadfoot	Dennis Burnett
John Calvey	Jimmy Carter	Phil Coleman
Bill 'Wiggy' Davis	Alf Dean	Sammy Frost
Archie Garrett	Frank Hancock	Neil Harris
Dean Horrix	Terry Hurlock	Johnny Johnson
Dick Jones	Willie Jones	John 'Tiny' Joyce
Tony Kinsella	Billy Martin	Dave Mehmet
Arthur Millar	Archie McKenzie	Alan McLeary
Terry McQuade	Kevin O'Callaghan	Jimmy Riley
Andy Roberts	Hugh Robertson	Neil Ruddock
Barry Salvage	Bobby Shinton	Lindsay Smith
Albert Sutherland	Liam Trotter	Darren Ward
Alan Welsh		

HOME-GROWN

Here's a Millwall team of home-grown talent that would fetch a
pretty penny in today's over-inflated transfer market:

1.	Brian Horne	7.	Joe Broadfoot
2.	Alan Dunne	8.	Dave Mehmet
3.	Ben Thatcher	9.	Teddy Sheringham
4.	Andy Roberts	10.	Mark Kennedy
5.	Barry Kitchener	11.	Kevin O'Callaghan
6.	Dave Harper		

Manager: Keith Stevens

BEST NICKNAMES XIs

Nicknames for footballers nowadays are normally a play on their surnames, such as Robbo (Paul Robinson) or Dunney (Alan Dunne), however, some still get labelled by the way they play or from a physical attribute. Here are two Millwall teams comprising players who were widely known by nicknames provided by the supporters down the years.

Tiny (John Joyce)	1	Denzil (Tony Warner)
Gilly (John Gilchrist)	2	Shaggy (Matt Lawrence)
Flint (Bill McCullough)	3	Razor (Neil Ruddock)
Snowball (Sammy Frost)	4	Warlock (Terry Hurlcok)
Chisel (Jimmy Forsyth)	5	Lurch (Barry Kitchener)
Banger (Billy Voisey)	6	Rhino (Keith Stevens)
Brown Bomber (Frank Neary)	7	Chicken George (George Lawrence)
Peanut (Wilf Phillips)	8	Fizzer (Nick Chatterton)
Percy (Bryan Conlon)	9	Chopper/Bomber (Neil Harris)
Tramcar (Fred Ramscar)	10	Elvis (Jon Goodman)
Rabbit (Charlie Elliott)	11	Merlin (Gordon Hill)

In his first spell with Millwall, central defender Darren Ward was known as the 'Peckham Beckham', while locally born half-back Fred Martin was referred to as the 'Bermondsey Bruiser' during his time at The Den.

MR PLOD

Besides goalkeeper Jimmy Carter (1896/97), three known Millwall players have also been members of the police force. The first was the capable Carter, whose one season saw him play 33 times. After his playing career finished he returned to his hometown of Preston when he became a member of the local constabulary until 1926.

Irishman Billy Murphy, who made just four appearances for the Lions in the last Southern League season of 1919/20, served in both 'F' and 'Y' Divisions of the Metropolitan Police.

Centre-forward Jim Ryan was also a member of the Met and was signed from Charlton Athletic for £3,000 in February 1965 to boost the Lions' shot-shy attack. But after 13 appearances and three goals he was on his way out of The Den by the following November. It was later reported that he became a male model.

THE EX-FACTOR

Since moving to the New Den in 1993, nine Millwall players have scored against one or the other of their former clubs in the league. They are:

Date	Player	Result
26/12/2001	Steve Claridge	Millwall 3–0 Crystal Palace
17/1/2004	Danny Dichio (2)	Millwall 2–1 Sunderland
12/4/2004	Danny Dichio	Millwall 1–1 West Brom
13/9/2005	Jermaine Wright	Wolves 1–2 Millwall
1/1/2007	Darren Byfield (3)	Millwall 4–1 Gillingham
20/1/2007	Darren Byfield (2)	Millwall 4–0 Rotherham
7/4/2007	Neil Harris	Millwall 1–0 Nottm Forest
23/2/2008	Marc Laird	Millwall 1–0 Port Vale
25/4/2009	Gary Alexander	Millwall 2–1 Leyton Orient
13/3/2010	Darren Ward	Millwall 4–0 Charlton Ath
13/4/2010	Jon Obika	Yeovil Town 1–1 Millwall

THE MAGNIFICENT SEVEN

When Millwall surpassed Reading's 30-year-old record of 55 home games without defeat in the autumn of 1966, the *London Evening Standard* afforded seven of the record-breaking team the accolade of Player of the Month for November.

The seven recipients of the award, presented by Football League President Len Shipman before the home match against Bolton Wanderers, were skipper Bryan Snowdon, fellow defenders Johnny Gilchrist, Harry Cripps and Tommy Wilson, midfielder Kenny Jones and forwards Lennie Julians and Billy Neil.

This septet was the mainstay of the run that would finally finish on 59 games, of which Tommy Wilson appeared in 55 of them followed by his fellow Scot John Gilchrist with 52. Left-back Harry Cripps played in 50 of the games, while Bryan Snowdon made 43 starts. Kenny Jones chalked up an admirable 47 games in midfield.

Of the forwards the excellent Len Julians played on 51 occasions while outside-left Billy Neil began 39 games. The only other substantial contribution came from former goalkeeper Alex Stepney who weighed in with 46 appearances before his transfer to Chelsea in the summer of 1966.

WARTIME ANARCHY

An incident occurred during a Crystal Palace v Millwall South Regional League fixture at Selhurst Park on 28 September 1940, when Palace were awarded a penalty in the 39th minute. The referee, Mr Reed, had adjudged that Jimmy Forsyth had deliberately fouled a Palace forward in the area.

The official was immediately surrounded by several Millwall players, including Forsyth, George Williams and Ted Smith, who showed and expressed their feelings (or dissent if you are a referee) at the decision. It was then that the Lions' skipper and a future manager, Reg (J.R.) Smith ran from his position to inform Reed 'You are not refereeing fairly.'

In reply the official asked for the captain's name, which was promptly answered by 'Smith, J.R.', who then turned to thump the ball from the penalty spot and into the crowd. Without further discussion Reed ordered Smith to take an early bath for deliberate and persistent misconduct. Smith refused to go and threatened to take his team with him.

The only alternative left to the flustered official was to suspend play and return to his dressing room. It was then that officials of both Millwall and Palace went to see Reed, who told them that he had sent Smith off, and that he had refused to go. One official asked him if he would continue with the match without JR? He said was prepared to resume the game if this was the case. The match restarted with the penalty being taken and the game reached its conclusion without further controversy.

The referee, in his opinion, felt that Smith's conduct was unjustifiable, reprehensible and deserving of the severest punishment given that he'd brought the game, the league and Millwall into disrepute. Incidentally, Palace won the game 2–1, with Freddie Fisher scoring for the Lions.

A GENTLEMAN AND A SCHOLAR

One of the greatest players to assist Millwall Athletic in the late Victorian and early Edwardian eras was J.H. (Joe) Gettins, who became the only player to appear in the club's FA Cup semi-finals of 1900 and 1903. A member of the famous Corinthians club, with whom he toured South Africa in 1897. Joe retained his amateur status throughout his career.

Joe's association with Millwall began back at Easter 1894 when he appeared in some friendly matches and he would play his final games for the club around his 30th birthday in November 1904. He was born in Middlesbrough in 1874 and was member of Middlesbrough's FA Amateur Cup-winning team in 1895 when they defeated the holders Old Carthusians 2–1 at Leeds. Due to his teaching commitments Joe would appear in 118 games and score 59 goals. Such was his standing with the professionals at Millwall, they presented him with gold-mounted umbrella on his 24th birthday. Another stroke of good fortune for Millwall was when Joe introduced Jack Calvey to the club in 1895.

His road into full-time educational came when he studied at Isleworth Training College (later Borough Road) and the

University of London, and after qualification he held various teaching posts between 1899 and 1907. He was later to become Professor of Education at University College Reading, from where he was given special dispensation (an afternoon off) to play for Millwall in an FA Cup third round second replay against Aston Villa at Reading's Elm Park ground. Around August 1910 Joe accepted the nomination as vice-president of the newly formed Millwall Football Supporters' Club.

When the First World War began, Joe donned the khaki as a member of the Royal Army Service Corps Territorial Force where he held the rank of captain from 1914 and was made temporary major in 1915. He was awarded the DSO on 3 June 1918 for distinction in military operations in France and Flanders. After the cessation of hostilities he became the bursar at the University of Liverpool on a salary of £700 per annum in June 1920, but Joe's stay there was short-lived as he resigned in November that year. It was then that Joe resumed his connection with the Army with an appointment with the War Office in 1921.

He became the chief of education at Sandhurst six years later, in 1927, and was appointed the Education Officer, Eastern Command, from 1931 until his retirement in 1933, the year Joe was awarded an OBE. He also commanded the Army School of Education at Shorncliffe and would reach the rank of Lieutenant-Colonel. In 1929 his book *Some Chapters on Writing English* was published and he also edited a volume on military conversations and correspondence in French.

In March 1938 he appeared on BBC radio show called *Spelling Bee* in which he was part of the Great Britain team that competed against the USA. Contestants were given 30 seconds to spell a particular word and points were won and lost if a team member was correct or not with their spelling. Needless to say Joe's team won by 37 points to the Americans' 27.

Joe was not only a splendid footballer but useful wicketkeeper/ batsman in the summer game – cycling was another pursuit, as was rowing. Many more words could be written about him, but space prevents it. Joseph Holmes Gettins passed away at his home in East Molesey, Surrey, in June 1954.

DO NOT ...

In 1924/25 Millwall, in their official match programme, offered some hints to fans on how to behave in a way that would today seem overbearing and schoolmasterly. Some of the don'ts are listed below:

DON'T make what may appear to you and your friends, 'funny' remarks respecting our own or visiting players. Such are not asked for by the Directors or players. Remember there are other quite as funny people as you present, who wish to follow the game.

DON'T give advice to the Referee. He has to give his decision quickly, and like the rest of us, makes mistakes. Always respect his decision; the game itself will be much better for doing so. There is plenty of room for good and reliable Referees. Why not try and pass for one yourself? It is by no means an easy job.

DON'T advise the players how to play or what to do. The players engaged by the Directors will doubtless have had some previous experience of the game. They are taking all the risks; you, personally, are quite safe behind the touchline.

DON'T forget our players have to face their opponents on the latter's ground. It is not always very difficult to get a little, at any rate, of your own back on your own ground.

These 'hints' are just a few of the those published, and given the crowd trouble we've experienced at The Den it appears these pieces of advice were generally ignored or forgotten by a section of the support.

TERRIBLE RUNS

Five seasons spring to mind where Millwall had terrible runs.

The 1933/34 season saw the Lions sent down on the last day of the campaign and their winless run of 11 matches from 29 January until 7 April included five draws; a victory in just one of those fixtures might have saved Millwall from the drop.

Twenty-four years later in the 1957/58 season the Lions produced another 11-match run without a success – it saw them score in all but two of their games between 11 January and 17 March, but they lost seven encounters in the process. In 1963/64 the drastic run endured by players and fans alike was a 10-game sequence that began on 26 August and ended with a 3–2 win at Peterborough on 7 October. They were testing times – Millwall managed just four goals (one an own goal) while conceding 21, and they lost 8 of the 10 matches played, failing to find the net in 7 of them.

The 1978/79 season got off to fine start when Millwall defeated Newcastle United on the opening day 2–1. It would be 13 weeks before the aroma of success next visited The Den with a 3–0 victory over Stoke City. The intervening period had been pure purgatory for the Lions faithful with a run of 13 games without a win, including 10 defeats.

One of most frustrating campaigns at Zampa Road has to be 1996/97, when after beating Luton Town on 8 March, Millwall went without a victory in the last 11 games. Again they managed just 4 goals in that time, 3 of which came at Wrexham in a 3–3 draw. In the last 6 fixtures the shot-shy strikers failed to score, though fortunately enough points had been gained to finish in mid-table.

GOAL RUNNERS

Goalscoring runs occasionally arrive from the most unlikely of sources. Nothing would illustrate this better than in the case of full-back Stan Anslow, who was selected to play at centre-forward against Crystal Palace at The Den in the FA Cup third round in January 1957. Thumping home a penalty, Stan set the Lions on their way to a 2–0 success. A week later, also at home, he registered a hat-trick in the 7–2 thrashing of Torquay United.

There came another goal against Palace the following week in a league match before he etched his name into Millwall history by scoring the two goals that defeated Newcastle United in the fourth round of the FA Cup. It didn't end there though – more came along in a 3–2 defeat at Brighton. So, in a run of 14 games in which he played as a striker, Stan hit an amazing 13 goals in just 8 matches.

The record for consecutive scoring is held by Steve Lovell, Millwall's Welsh international, with 13 goals in 11 games. He had previously been, like Anslow, a full-back, but also had appeared in midfield. Given the opportunity to play as the main striker in the absence of the injured Dean Neal, Steve's incredible run saw him register goals in all of Millwall's games during October and November 1984. His tally is listed below.

1.	2 October	Derby County	(H) 2–1	1 (penalty)
2.	6 October	Gillingham	(A) 4–1	1
3.	9 October	Chelsea	(H) 1–1	1 (League Cup)
4.	13 October	Brentford	(H) 2–0	2
5.	20 October	York City	(A) 1–1	1
6.	23 October	Lincoln City	(H) 2–0	2 (1 penalty)
7.	27 October	Bristol City	(H) 1–1	1
8.	10 November	Preston NE	(H) 3–0	1 (penalty)
9.	17 November	Weymouth	(A) 3–0	1 (FAC1)
10.	24 November	Bristol Rovers	(A) 1–1	1
11.	28 November	Bradford City	(A) 1–3	1

When centre-forward Pat Terry signed for Millwall in February 1962, he was seen as the final piece in the jigsaw in the push for promotion. He scored on his debut in a 3–2 victory at Chesterfield, but drew a blank against one of his former clubs, Gillingham, though he did find the net in his next 3 games.

Having registered 5 goals in 9 starts, Pat would then score in the next 6 fixtures (then a club record) in which Millwall lost just once. Millwall finally clinched the Fourth Division title with a 2–2 draw at Barrow and at the season's conclusion Pat's final tally was a very impressive 13 goals in 17 appearances.

A striker earlier in his career, Gordon Borland had been regarded more as an attacking midfielder at The Den, and was the previous holder the record. His 7-match run began on 10 February 1973 against Oxford United with a successful spot-kick and ended on 24 March in a 2–1 loss at Burnley. In his run Gordon netted on 9 occasions which included 2 penalties.

At the start of the 1903/04 season skipper Ben Hulse scored in the first 6 Southern League fixtures, scoring 8 times. Another captain, Joe Wilson scored with 3 successive penalty-kicks in 1911/12 versus New Brompton, Exeter City and Brentford, and later that season scored in 4 games on the trot, 3 of which came from spot-kicks.

During the 1913/14 campaign Welshman Wally Davis scored a brace in 3 consecutive games against Bristol Rovers, Merthyr and Plymouth Argyle, while Joe Walters became the first Lion to score in 4 successive matches in the Football League in the 1921/22 season.

A SOLDIER'S TALE – PART TWO

Trooper John Fitzpatrick of the 8th Royal Irish Hussars had some unfortunate times during his football career, having made his Southern League debut for Millwall Athletic in the 3–2 home defeat by Southampton in November 1897. He was later that season selected for the home FA Cup match against Sheppey United which Millwall won handsomely 5–1.

It was then his troubles began when he was found to be ineligible to play. The upshot of this oversight was the Football Association decided the match should be replayed, this time at Sheppey. There was to be no reprieve for Millwall who meekly went out to a revitalised Sheppey United who rattled home 5 goals without reply.

John would appear for Millwall over the next 3 years when Army commitments allowed and his last game was against Thames Ironworks just before Christmas 1899. A further stoke of misfortune befell him and Millwall saw the game abandoned after 69 minutes owing to fog enveloping the Ironworks ground at Canning Town.

This all took place before he fell foul of the authorities yet again. Even before a ball was kicked in the 1899/1900 season, he signed professional registration forms for Notts County without a transfer taking place, as he was still registered as a Millwall player. His registration with County was then declared void and any money paid to him by Notts County had to be refunded. Insult was added to injury when he was suspended until 1 October 1899.

After these mishaps it would appear John decided he was more suited to remain a regular soldier, and he would later serve in the Boer War (1899–1902).

ULSTER SUPPLY

Not too many players from Northern Ireland have plied their trade at The Den but listed here are eleven of the best.

1.	Ted Hinton	(1949–52)
2.	Des Quinn	(1949–55)
3.	Billy McCullough	(1966–7)
4.	Tom Brolly	(1935–50)
5.	Gerry Bowler	(1950–5)
6.	Walter McMillen	(1946–50)
7.	Bryan Hamilton	(1977–9)
8.	Chris McGrath	(1975–6)
9.	Gerry Armstrong	(1986–7)
10.	Ray Gough	(1964–5)
11.	Ian Stewart	(1982–3)

Manager: Billy McCracken (1933–6)

NEEDED: A 20-GOALS-A-SEASON STRIKER!

There have been no less than 23 players who have managed to score 20 or more Southern/Football League goals in a season. The full list so far is:

Player	Season	Goals
Alf Twigg	1906/07	27
Wally Davis	1912/13	23
Jimmy Broad	1919/20	32
Dick Parker	1926/27	37
John Landells	1927/28	33
Wilf Phillips	1927/28	27
Jack Cock	1927/28	25
Jack Cock	1928/29	22
Jimmy Constantine	1948/49	23
Jimmy Constantine	1950/51	26
Johnny Summers	1955/56	24
Peter Burridge	1960/61	35
Dave Jones	1960/61	24
Peter Burridge	1961/62	23
Dave Jones	1961/62	22
Lennie Julians	1965/66	22
Alf Wood	1973/74	21
Steve Lovell	1984/85	21
Teddy Sheringham	1987/88	22
Tony Cascarino	1987/88	20
Teddy Sheringham	1990/91	33
Neil Harris	1999/2000	25
Neil Harris	2000/01	28
Steve Morison	2009/10	20

AN UNFORTUNATE SOUL

When Millwall signed Scottish Under-21 international Gerard Lavin from Watford for around £400,000 in November 1995 it appeared they had signed a quality player who could perform at right-back or in midfield.

The Lions were riding high in Division One with just 2 defeats in 18 matches, but when Gerard made his debut in the 19th game (against Stoke City) Millwall promptly lost the next 5 fixtures in which Lavin played. The next 2 saw a draw and another loss and following another winless streak he finally found himself involved in a victory against Norwich City at The Den the following February – some three months later.

Millwall's plight had become serious and after leading the table at Christmas they now found themselves embroiled in a relegation dogfight. Gerard's next run in the team saw just 2 victories in 8 games. However, he was missing when the ignominy of relegation was confirmed on the last day of the season, with Millwall needing a victory at Ipswich Town and only managing a 0–0 draw.

So in his first 20 games, Millwall had lost 14. Nagging injuries restricted his appearances in his second season to just 9 and nor was he seen much in 1997/98, appearing in only the last 7 games (which Millwall failed to win any of). Gerard's redemption came in his last campaign at The Den (1998/99) where he made 38 starts that culminated in a Wembley appearance in the Auto Windscreens Trophy. Millwall lost that game too.

UNBEATEN AT HOME

Millwall have managed to remain unbeaten at home on seven occasions in their history and in all bar one of those campaigns (1971/72), they either won the title or were promoted. The list is as follows:

	P	W	D	
1894/95	8	8	0	Champions (Southern League)
1895/96	9	9	0	Champions (Southern League)
1927/28	21	19	2	Champions (Third Division S)
1964/65	23	13	10	Runners-Up (Fourth Division)
1965/66	23	19	4	Runners-Up (Third Division)
1971/72	21	14	7	
1984/85	23	18	5	Runners-Up (Third Division)

AN INTERNATIONAL SCARE

The glamorous world of international football can sometimes have a sinister side, as Lion Marc Bircham would testify. Through having a Canadian grandfather, he became eligible to play for their national side, gaining his first cap against Northern Ireland at Belfast in April 1999 in which he scored in a 1–1 draw. Marc would go on to establish himself as a regular in the team with a string of impressive performances in friendlies and World Cup qualifying games in Toronto and Edmonton.

But it was after one particular match against Guatemala that Marc's problem arose. Canada had beaten the Central Americans 1–0 and Marc won the man of the match award. The following day the Canadian FA received some correspondence threatening Bircham's life. Ominously Marc was placed under armed guard as maps were issued to the police indicating possible assassination points at the stadium where Canada were due to play.

Eventually nothing came of the threats and Marc appeared to take all this drama in his stride, but was quoted as saying, 'No matter how much I love playing international football, I won't be going to Guatemala.'

HOMESICKNESS

Striker Theo Robinson's brief encounter with Millwall lasted for 12 games and 3 goals and came to an end in February 2011, with Theo stating that he could not settle in South-East London and was feeling homesick. This resulted in a transfer to Derby County so that he could be nearer his family in Birmingham.

However, Theo is not the first and certainly won't be the last player to have suffered this. A similar occurrence at The Den arose in 1953 when forward Alan Monkhouse failed to return to Millwall after he was given leave to visit his home in Stockton-on-Tees.

Alan said he was homesick and unhappy and had no intention of returning to London, and although he had no complaints against the club, he threatened to quit football if he could not get a transfer. Where Monkhouse and Robinson's situations differ is the length of time they were at The Den. Theo was there for a matter of months, whereas Alan had been a Millwall player for over four years.

He eventually got a dream move to Newcastle United in October 1953 and would score 8 times in 14 games in his first season as a Magpie. Following spells with York City and South Shields Alan, ironically, found himself moving back south to join Dartford in August 1959.

CONSECUTIVE APPEARANCES

The man who currently holds the record for the most consecutive appearances in a Millwall shirt is former captain and centre-half Barry Kitchener, who cobbled together 213 league and cup starts between 1968 and 1973. Kitch, a product of the Lions' youth system, missed the League Cup replay against Barnsley in September 1968 but went on an unbroken run afterwards which only came to an end following his appearance in the home victory over Luton Town on 26 February 1973.

If one goes solely on Football League appearances then Barry's total leaps to an impressive 244 consecutive matches. He currently holds the all-time appearance records for Millwall in all competitions.

EIGHT GREAT GATES

The eight biggest attendances (over 50,000) the Lions have performed in front of are as follows:

90,000   v Chelsea (Football League South final),
              April 1945

73,168   v Swindon Town (League One play-off final),
               May 2010
71,350   v Manchester United (FA Cup final), May 2004
62,813   v Sunderland (FA Cup semi-final), April 1937
59,661   v Scunthorpe United (Football League play-off final),
               May 2009
58,189   v Tottenham Hotspur (A) (FA Cup third round replay),
               February 1967
56,112   v Sunderland (FA Cup semi-final), April 2004
55,349   v Wigan Athletic (Auto Windscreens Shield final),
               April 1999

DURABILITY

A Millwall record that seems unlikely to be surpassed in today's
football is the label of an ever-present. A player would have to be
super-fit, maintain a level of consistency and not fall foul of a card-
waving referee to rack up this status over a season (or seasons).
However, Millwall's John 'Tiny' Joyce appeared to have at least
two of these qualities in abundance and in the 1901/02 season he
appeared in all 56 games that the club played.

'Tiny' was ever-present in 30 Southern League fixtures, 16 in the
Western League and 8 in the London League (in which he kept 17
clean sheets) as well as 2 FA Cup ties.

This test of durability stood for 72 years when in 1983/84, the
equally hard-wearing Welshman Steve Lovell was unmoveable for
57 matches. This figure comprised all 46 in the Football League
plus 11 games in the FA Cup, League Cup and the Associate
Members' Cup.

HEAVYWEIGHT LIONS

Here is a formidable selection of the heaviest Lions to wear the
XXL shirt with distinction, six of whom are worthy net-minders:

John 'Tiny' Joyce	16st 0lb	1900–02 & 1903–1910
Mark Crossley	16st 0lb	1997–98
Fred Griffiths	15st 0lb	1900–01
Poul Hübertz	14st 9lb	2006–07
Paul Jones	14st 8lb	2005–06
Nigel Spink	14st 6lb	1997–2000
Trevor Aylott	14st 0lb	1982–83
Dave Cusack	13st 12lb	1982–85
Bob Peeters	13st 12lb	2003–06
Tim Carter	13st 11lb	1993–98
Sam Allardyce	13st 10lb	1981–83
Sid Heaton	13st 9lb	1905–06
David Forde	13st 7lb	2008–
Danny Chapman	13st 6lb	1994–95
Jim Jeffrey	13st 6lb	1908–13

A GALLANT MAN

Billy 'Banger' Voisey was Millwall born and bred and became the recipient of two gallantry awards in February 1922 for his deeds during the First World War. Bill was to be presented with two medals by the Mayor of Poplar prior to a borough council meeting.

Bill had joined Millwall in 1908 but had to wait until December 1910 before making his debut in the home match against Southend United. By the time hostilities broke out in 1914 'Banger' had appeared in over 80 Southern League matches.

During the conflict Bill served with 187th Brigade of the Royal Field Artillery, often acting as Battery Sergeant-Major where he displayed marked gallantry and resourcefulness. One particular case arose in March 1918 when the battery's ordered retirement saw them sustain heavy casualties. Bill's fine example and leadership was conducted with no shortage of courage and was displayed with a cheery disposition.

For this Bill was awarded the DCM and for bravery in the field was further awarded the Military Medal. The mayor then handed the 'gongs' to Billy who then asked to convey his thanks to the council for being allowed to receive the medals publicly. Not only did this son of Millwall receive his own nation's gratitude but also that of Belgium who bestowed upon him the Croix de Guerre.

Billy won a single cap for England in a Victory international against Wales in 1919 and was the first goalscorer in the Football League for Millwall when the Lions defeated Bristol Rovers 2–0 at The Den in August 1920.

MINI LIONS

Here are some of those Millwall bundles of energy who maybe vertically challenged, but who confirm that all good things come in small packages:

Peter Banks	5ft 1in	1891–3
Steve Adams	5ft 4in	1977–8
Daniel Aitken	5ft 4in	1906–7
Joe Hutton	5ft 4in	1958–60
Mickey Weir	5ft 4in	1995–6
Teddy Bassett	5ft 5in	1911–12
Alf Dean	5ft 5in	1906–7 & 1908–9
Freddie Fisher	5ft 5in	1938–9
Alf Geddes	5ft 5in	1894–9
Danny Wallace	5ft 5in	1992–3
Chris Clarke	5ft 5¼in	1964–6
Terry Brisley	5ft 6in	1975–8
Les Briley	5ft 6in	1984–91

THE SWEET SMELL OF THE EAST FERRY ROAD

Fred Pelly of Old Foresters, Casuals and the Corinthians, who won three England caps in the mid-1890s, had appeared on a few occasions on Millwall's ground at the East Ferry Road for various teams and as a true-blue amateur left-back, revelled in the physical side of the game. However, Fred's biggest complaint after appearing at Millwall was not the hurly-burly or the rough play, nor was his being dumped on his backside when tackled . . . what really irked him the most was that he had to carry the smell around with him for weeks allegedly. Whatever had lain on the surface of the pitch is open to question and we can only sympathise with the 6ft tall Fred because the 'pong' he inherited had a 15 stone frame to linger upon.

OF INDEPENDENT MEANS

When 17-year-old midfield player Tom Kilbey replaced Alan Dunne to make his first start for Millwall in the Johnstone's Paint Trophy fixture at Swansea in September 2007, he became the third known Lion after Neil Harris (Brentwood) and Andy Frampton (Lancing) to appear in the first team following an education at a public school.

Tom had been educated Forest School and had represented the Independent Schools' FA Under-16 team. Sadly, the Swansea game was Tom's only match for the Lions, as he was transferred to Portsmouth shortly afterwards.

THE FEEL OF MONEY

In these days of the cash-flushed Premiership and multi-million pound transfers two salaries from nearly 50 years ago show how football has moved on financially. For in December 1962 Millwall's Manager Ron Gray was on £1,346 per annum while Secretary Gordon Borland was paid £1,016 over the same period. Even so, broken down on a weekly basis, Ron's £25 and Borland's £19-plus would be regarded as a good week's pay back in 1962.

TWELVE OF THE BEST

On their way to retaining the Southern League championship in 1896 Millwall set a club record of 12 consecutive wins, which are listed here:

1895

26/10/1895	Reading (H)	2–0
	J. Matthew, Leatherbarrow	
9/11/1895	Chatham (H)	6–3
	W. Jones, Leatherbarrow, Geddes (2) Malloch, Whelan	
16/11/1895	Royal Ordnance (A)	1–0
	Geddes	
30/11/1895	Clapton (H)	11–1
	Geddes, W. Jones (2), Leatherbarrow (3), Malloch, Whelan (2), King, opponent own goal	
7/12/1895	Luton T (A)	3–0
	Gettins (2), Whelan	
21/12/1895	Clapton (A)	5–0
	Malloch (4), Whelan	

1896

18/1/1896	New Brompton (A)	2–1
	Geddes (2)	
8/2/1896	Reading (A)	4–2
	Gettins (3), Malloch	
15/2/1896	Ilford (H)	8–1
	Calvey (3), King, Gettins (2), Malloch (2)	
20/2/1896	Ilford (A)	4–2
	Calvey, Geddes, Malloch, Whelan	
22/2/1896	Chatham (A)	2–1
	Calvey (pen), Whelan	
14/3/1896	Royal Ordnance (H)	4–0
	Gettins (2), Calvey, opponent own goal	

While the best in the Football League came in 1928 when Millwall marched towards the Third Division South championship, with 10 consecutive wins that are listed here:

1928

10/3/1928	QPR (H)	6–1
	Phillips (2), Landells, Bryant, Cock (2)	
17/3/1928	Watford (A)	3–0
	Cock, Phillips (2)	
24/3/1928	Newport C (H)	5–1
	Cock (4), Phillips	
31/3/1928	Coventry City (A)	3–0
	Chance, Black, Bryant	
6/4/1928	Exeter City (H)	2–0
	Black, Phillips	
7/4/1928	Merthyr T (H)	3–0
	Landells (2), Cock	
9/4/1928	Exeter City (A)	4–2
	Landells, Black, Chance, Bryant	
14/4/1928	Walsall (A)	5–2
	Landells (3), Black, Cock	
21/4/1928	Gillingham (H)	6–0
	Phillips (2), Cock (3), Bryant	
25/4/1928	Gillingham (A)	1–0
	Cock	

WHEN LION MET IRON

The recent history and rivalry between Millwall and West Ham United has been well documented over the last 40 years, but tension and disorder is nothing new between the two and one has to refer back to 1906 to find when the seeds of future confrontations were sown. The events of unrest began at Upton Park on 17 September for the opening Western League game of the season.

Hardly had the game begun when the first incident took place. Hammers wing-half Len Jarvis (or Dick as he was popularly known) came up against Millwall's outside-right Alf Dean and in the ensuing tussle Alf was hurled violently against the surrounding railings and suffered injuries that forced him to miss the rest of the game.

Millwall's centre-half George Comrie became the Lions' second casualty when he collided with one of the pavilion supports and he too left the field of play, leaving Millwall to soldier on with 9 men. Other stoppages for petty infringements interrupted the flow of the game and the spectators were getting agitated. This led to a free-for-all that intensified at the Castle Street end. Amid all the mayhem some light relief appeared in the shape of a small dog and for a while it put everyone in relative good humour.

Where the canine intruder had come from no one knew, but wherever the ball travelled, so did the dog. Eventually the referee, Mr E. Case of Cheshire, halted the game, and the dog, which was vigorously wagging its tail, evaded all attempts at capture. Even Millwall goalkeeper 'Tiny' Joyce failed to coax the animal to come quietly. While the spectators were roaring with laughter the dog seemed to get bored with the proceedings and calmly trotted through the pavilion gates, never to be seen again.

The dog incident had put the crowd in better spirits, but the ill-feeling generated by Dean's injury diluted any further excitement on the resumption of play. The Lions had done exceedingly well to hold out for so long but the pressure finally told when West Ham scored the only goal of the game. In keeping with what had gone on before it was a penalty, awarded in the second half to settle the outcome. George Kitchen, the West Ham goalkeeper, was entrusted with the spot-kick, which he successfully converted past his opposite number 'Tiny' Joyce.

The result of what went on that day went before the Football Association, who decided that the referee failed to properly control the game, and was suspended for the rest of the season. The instigator, Len Jarvis, was suspended for 14 days from 30 October for what was deemed a serious foul on Alf Dean. The players of both sides were censured and warned about their future conduct.

FA CUP ODDITIES

Millwall held an unenviable record of 24 unsuccessful attempts to win a FA Cup tie away from home. It lasted from 1951/52 to 1971/72. Success finally arrived with a 2–0 victory at Everton in February 1973. Coincidentally, the season in which the Lions ended their hoodoo, Stoke City began their unwanted run which also spanned 24 games before ending in 1992/93.

Dennis Wise is one of four players to appear in an FA Cup final with three different clubs: Wimbledon (1988), Chelsea (1994, 1997 and 2003) and Millwall (2004).

Curtis Weston became the youngest player to appear in the final against Manchester United on 22 May 2004, while former Lion Paul Allen was the youngest player to appear in a Wembley Final at 17 years, 256 days for West Ham United versus Arsenal on 10 May 1980.

Millwall are one of four clubs who in their non-league days managed to knock out the current Football League champions. Millwall achieved this by defeating Aston Villa in a second replay in 1900.

John Sutcliffe, Millwall's goalkeeper in the 1903 semi-final, is joint-holder with his brother Charles Sutcliffe, as the brothers to appear in an FA Cup final with longest span of time between the finals. John, who was born in 1868, appeared for Bolton Wanders in their 4–1 defeat to Notts County in 1894 when Charles was three years old. Latterly Charles would also take up the game of football and like his elder sibling, he too became a goalkeeper. His appearance came at Wembley in 1925 when his Sheffield United team beat Cardiff City 1–0. The length of time was an amazing 31 years and it is a record that will surely not be surpassed.

Two former Lions, Clive Allen (1993–94) and Paul Allen (1997–98), are one of the few examples of cousins appearing together in a cup final. It came in 1987 when their Tottenham team were beaten by Coventry City 3–2.

JRs x 2

Since 1935 the Millwall supporters had been delighted by the play of outside-left J.R. 'Reggie' Smith after he joined from Hitchin Town. However, in March 1938 the Lions signed another J.R. – this one was James Robert Richardson from Newcastle United for a then record fee of £4,000.

Jimmy Richardson had won two caps for England in 1933 and began his full-time career with the Magpies in 1928, but he became the focus of attention in the 1932 FA Cup final when Newcastle beat the Arsenal 2–1 with his infamous 'over the line goal'. It occurred when Jimmy chased a long clearance down the right and sliding on the lush Wembley turf, managed to retrieve the ball although it appeared to have gone a foot over the byline, after which he centred a pinpoint cross for Jack Allen to head home. The Arsenal defence, having eased up, assumed the goal would be disallowed, but were horrified to see the referee pointing to the middle.

After United's relegation in 1934 he was sold to First Division Huddersfield Town in the following October. He spent three years in Yorkshire before moving back to Newcastle in 1937. His stay back on Tyneside, though, lasted a mere five months before his transfer to The Den. So within a year Jim had appeared in Divisions One, Two and Three and then Two again following Millwall's promotion in May 1938.

WHAT'S IN A NAME?

There have been some unusual and quaint names at Millwall over the years and here are a few examples:

GENERAL Stevenson	1903–11
John SKIDMORE Gilchrist	1960–9
Gerry COLUMBIA Bowler	1950–5
BARRINGTON Hayles	2004–6
Harry Barker HANKEY	1922–4

FOSTER Hedley	1937–9
VIVIAN Woodward	1946–8
Arthur LONGBOTTOM	1962–3
HARTLEY Shutt	1900–1
HILLARY Griffiths	1905–6

LIONS AT LENGTH

Some of the lanky boys who have represented the Lions over the years:

Poul Hübertz	6ft 5in	2006–7
Sergei Baltacha	6ft 5in	2002–3
Bob Peeters	6ft 5in	2003–6
Colin Doyle	6ft 5in	2005–6
Jim Harrold	6ft 3½in	1923–4
Joe Dolan	6ft 3in	1998–2004
Chris Day	6ft 3in	2006–8
Rob Douglas	6ft 3in	2007–8
Jens Berthel Askou	6ft 3in	2010–11
Danny Dichio	6ft 3in	2003–5

HERR SCHMIDT

Down the years Millwall have had a shed load of players named Smith in their ranks, but one was definitely (and the other allegedly) born with the German equivalent of Smith – Schmidt. The first was James Christopher Reginald (aka 'JR' or 'Reggie') who became a Lion in 1935 and would serve Millwall as a player until 1946 when he transferred to Dundee.

His father had supposedly been a South African Springbok rugby international who toured the British Isles and decided to stay. However, and according to his birth certificate, Reg was born

Smith at Battersea in 1912, with the father's name is given as Frank Smith. Also, there appears to have been no South African rugby international named Frank Smith. At The Den this hard-shooting and speedy outside-left became a firm favourite and was capped twice by England in 1938. He later became Millwall manager in 1959.

The other Herr Schmidt is Wilf Smith who was actually born in Neumünster in the old West Germany in September 1946. His family took the English version of the name shortly after arriving in Britain with their young son. Wilf too, would be honoured by his country when he appeared on 6 occasions for the England Under-23 side. Although he only played 5 times for Millwall after joining in January 1975, he made a favourable impression with the supporters who would have liked to have seen Wilf as a permanent signing.

Unfortunately, he returned to Coventry City following his loan spell at The Den without a deal being struck. He was, however, transferred the following March, to Bristol Rovers, and when he returned to Cold Blow Lane for the last game of the 1974/75 season with Rovers, Wilf was given a very warm welcome by the Lions supporters.

ALL SAINTS' DAYS

Incredible as it may seem, Millwall have failed to register a win over Southampton in any of the 12 FA Cup or League Cup meetings they've taken part in. In 9 matches in the FA Cup (dating back to 1900) Millwall have scored just 3 goals. The nearest the Lions came to laying this particular ghost came at St Mary's in 2003 when Southampton equalised in the 90th minute through Kevin Davies, who had been on loan at The Den earlier that season. Inevitably Millwall lost the replay.

The 3 League Cup games have also proved barren, with Millwall not scoring a single goal. Here, too, the nearest Millwall came to beating the Saints saw the Lions go out in a penalty shoot-out in 1985. Here's the full list of these annoying statistics:

FA Cup	1899/1900	0–0	replay	0–3
	1904/05	1–3		
	1926–27	0–0	replay	0–2
	1985/86	0–0	replay	0–1
	2002/03	1–1	replay	1–2
League Cup	1985/86	0–0	2nd leg	0–0 over two legs lost on penalties
	2006/07	0–4		

JANUARY SALE!

In January 1970 news broke that would have gladdened the hearts of many Millwall supporters. The Bermondsey-born showbiz personality Tommy Steele was linked with taking over as chairman of the club from the unpopular incumbent Mickey Purser, whose motor car showrooms along the Old Kent Road had regularly been a target for disgruntled fans. The latest attack on his business, in December 1969, came following the home defeat by Cardiff City.

Tommy, who was then appearing at the London Palladium, had written to the club, and the letter was published in full in the *Daily Express*. He also had the backing of the only female boxing promoter in Britain – the glamorous blonde Beryl Cameron Gibbons who was also the landlady of the famous Thomas A' Beckett pub then an Old Kent Road landmark.

Even the hard-nosed secretary of the Football League, Alan Hardaker, voiced his opinion that, 'The game needs men with money and ideas.' Another individual interested in acquiring Millwall was Essex businessman Stan Canter, who had made more than one move to purchase Purser's shares. However much Steele and Canter were willing to pay it appeared not to be enough for Purser to sell. The negotiations with the interested parties ended without resolve, and it saw Purser remain at the helm until the autumn of 1974.

RELATIVELY SPEAKING

A sample of Millwall players with family ties and connections to other football clubs:

Wally Hinshelwood (1960–1) Father of **Paul** (Millwall 1984–7).

Leon Vaessen (1957–61) Father of **Paul** who famously scored Arsenal's winner against Juventus in 1980.

Scott Fitzgerald (1996–2001) Cousin of **Tony Gale** former Fulham, West Ham and Blackburn central defender.

Billy Neil (1963–72) Cousin of **Alex 'The Golden Vision' Young,** one of Everton's greatest players. Billy is also related to **Harry Thomson,** the former Burnley goalkeeper.

Sid Chedgzoy (1934–5) Son of the former Everton and England winger **Sam.**

Brian Clark (1973–5) Son of **Don Clark** who played for Bristol City.

John Colquhoun (1991–2) Son of **John** senior of Oldham and Scunthorpe fame.

Sergei Baltacha (2002–3) Son of **Sergei** senior of Ipswich and Dynamo Kiev.

Kevin Bremner (1982–5) Brother of **Des** of Aston Villa and Birmingham City.

Kenny Brown (1997–8) Son of **Ken** senior; West Ham centre-half.

Harry Earle (1889–2) Father of **Stan Earle** of West Ham and England.

Jermaine Wright (2005–6) Cousin of **Ian Wright** of Arsenal and England.

Darren Ward (2001–5, 2009–) Brother of **Elliott** of West Ham and Norwich.

THE HOT SHOT AND THE RED HOT MAMA

When skipper Dave Mangnall scored the first of his 49 Millwall goals against Bristol Rovers on his debut at The Den in August 1936 it was a double celebration for him. For on the previous day his wife had presented him with a son.

The guest of honour at the match was none other than the American actress and singer Sophie Tucker (1886–1966) who through her delivery of comical and somewhat risqué songs earned herself the nickname 'The Last of the Red Hot Mamas'. So enthralled by the game and no less of Mangnall's contribution, she was to become godmother to Dave's newly born son. However, Bristol Rovers went and spoiled the day by winning 2–1.

ET'S LANGUAGE

Millwall's versatile midfield performer Etienne Verveer (1991–4) was not only a talented footballer, but was also multilingual. He spoke six languages: Dutch, English, French, German, Indonesian and Surinamese.

HOME SWEET HOME

With a mushrooming of new stadia during the past 20 years or so, listed here are the defunct grounds that have featured on Millwall's itinerary since football resumed in 1946 and the Lions' last league appearance at the ground.

Opponent	Venue	Last visited
Accrington Stanley	Peel Park	1960
Arsenal	Highbury	1990
Barrow	Holker Street	1965
Bolton Wanderers	Burnden Park	1994
Bradford	Park Avenue	1965
Brighton & Hove Albion	Goldstone Ground	1991
Bristol Rovers	Eastville	1984
Cardiff City	Ninian Park	2006
Chester City	Sealand Road	1975
Chesterfield	Recreation Ground	2000
Colchester United	Layer Road	2001
Coventry City	Highfield Road	2004
Darlington	Feethams	1965
Derby County	Baseball Ground	1995
Doncaster Rovers	Belle Vue	1984
Gateshead	Redheugh Park	1960
Halifax Town	The Shay	1975
Huddersfield Town	Leeds Road	1987
Hull City	Boothferry Park	1988
Leicester City	Filbert Street	1996
Manchester City	Maine Road	1996
Middlesbrough	Ayresome Park	1994
Newport County	Somerton Park	1984
Northampton Town	County Ground	1967
Oxford United	Manor Ground	2001
Reading	Elm Park	1995
Rotherham United	Millmoor	2004
Scunthorpe United	Old Show Ground	1966
Shrewsbury Town	Gay Meadow	1997
Southampton	The Dell	1989
Stoke City	Victoria Ground	1995
Sunderland	Roker Park	1995
Swansea City	Vetch Field	1985
Walsall	Fellows Park	1984
Wigan Athletic	Springfield Park	1998
Wimbledon	Plough Lane	1989

MILLWALL'S TOP 10 FA CUP SCORERS

John Shepherd	15	Ken Burditt	7
Joe Gettins	10	John McLeod	7
Dave Mangnall	10	Jack Calvey	6
Alex McKenzie	8	Jack Cock	6
Frank Neary	8	Alex Rae	6

THE Os HAVE NOTHING

If Millwall's record against Southampton in both the major cup competitions is woeful, then their contests with London rivals Clapton/Leyton Orient in the same cups put the boot firmly on the other foot. In 11 matches, including two-legged ties, the Lions remain unbeaten. The games are:

1.	9 January 1915	FA Cup won 2–1
2.	13 January 1923	FA Cup won 2–0
3.	21 September 1976	League Cup drew 0–0
4.	12 October 1976	replay drew 0–0 aet
5.	19 October 1976	second replay (at Highbury) won 3–0
6.	2 September 1981	first round 1st leg drew 1–1
7.	16 September 1981	first round 2nd leg won 3–2
8.	18 August 1987	first round 1st leg drew 1–1
9.	25 August 1987	first round 2nd leg won 1–0
10.	18 August 1992	first round 1st leg drew 2–2
11.	26 August 1992	first round 2nd leg won 3–0

A MILLWALL GAZETTEER

A Lions team made up of place-names from around Britain:

Peter **Wells** (Somerset)
Alan **Slough** (Berkshire)

George **Eccles** (Lancashire)
Bryan **Hamilton** (Lanarkshire)
Mel **Blyth** (Northumberland)
Ron **Mansfield** (Nottinghamshire)
Tom **Brighton** (Sussex)
Teddy **Sheringham** (Norfolk)
John **Sutton** (Surrey)
Andy **Lincoln** (Lincolnshire)
Austin **Hayes** (Middlesex)

HOW MANY?

When a club struggles during the course of a season, the reasons can be plentiful: poor results, injuries, inconsistency and bad luck all play a part. However, another pointer is the amount of players used in the course of a season. High turnover of playing personnel often follows a change of manager – when the new boss has weighed up the situation he will generally discard some of the previous incumbent's players.

But the 2007/08 season takes some beating when Millwall used no less than 40 players in all competitions. Included in this number were 5 goalkeepers – a record for the Lions. The campaign commenced with Chris Day, whose tenure ended after 5 games following a 3–0 defeat at Brighton. The Scottish international Rob Douglas was then drafted in from Leicester City on loan and appeared in 7 games.

Former Chelsea goalkeeper Lenny Pidgeley became flavour of the month again for the next 13 fixtures, but lost out to January transfer window signing Rhys Evans from Blackpool. Rhys lasted 33 minutes into his third game when he was substituted by the fifth custodian of the season, Preston Edwards. An England youth international, Preston had been highly regarded but his brief cameo was to be his only league appearance for Millwall before being released.

After recovering, Evans regained his position between the sticks for the remainder of the season, but he too was let go in the summer of 2008. In contrast to these 5 net-minders, David Forde, the current Lions number one, has been ever-present in all but one of Millwall's first-team matches since he joined in 2008.

THE GRASS IS GREENER WHERE?

Here are some post-Second World War players who did very well after leaving Cold Blow Lane:

Irishman **Jimmy Dunne**, after one match for Millwall, went on to play in over 240 games for Torquay United in two spells at Plainmoor and 143 matches for Fulham. He was also capped by the Republic of Ireland.

After racking up 2 appearances for the Lions **John Richardson** would appear in over 300 league games for Brentford, Fulham and Aldershot.

Goalkeeper **Graham Brown** played one League Cup tie for Millwall in 1964, but went on to amass 142 starts for Mansfield Town from 1969 to 1973. He notched up another 157 appearances for Doncaster Rovers, Swansea City, York City and Rotherham United.

The hard-tackling **Pat Lally** found his path into the Millwall first team blocked and after just one game at The Den sought pastures new. He went on to make 357 league appearances at York City, Swansea City, Aldershot and Doncaster Rovers. Pat now works with the PFA in Manchester.

Walworth-born **Alan Garner** was, like Lally, released in the summer of 1971 and went on carve out a useful career with Watford (88 matches) followed by 200 starts at Luton Town before clocking up 36 appearances for Portsmouth. Alan started every one of his matches for all of his clubs.

Andy Donnelly, a 20-year-old goalkeeper, joined Millwall from Clyde in May 1963. Without making the first team he left the following year to join non-league Weymouth. After a two-year stint in Dorset he was snapped up by Torquay United in 1967, and in four years at Plainmoor clocked-up 160 league appearances.

Midfielder **Alan Welsh** had two attempts to make the grade at The Den, firstly in 1965 in which he became a prolific goalscorer for the reserves. In his five games for the first team Alan's potential deserted him and he was transferred to Torquay United where he immediately hit it off. Scoring 45 goals in 146 matches caught the eye of Plymouth Argyle in 1972 for whom he appeared 66 times. A move to Bournemouth saw him play 35 times before moving back to the Lions in 1975. However, a much more experienced Alan failed once again with just 1 goal in 9 matches.

Striker **Steve Torpey** was born in 1970 and made 7 appearances for Millwall. Following moves to Bradford, Swansea and Bristol (and latterly Scunthorpe United), his goalscoring, fitness and staying power saw him still plying his trade into his late thirties, well into the 21st century.

SUPER, SUPER NEIL, SUPER NEIL HARRIS!

Millwall legend and the club's leading overall goalscorer, Neil Harris can be justifiably proud of his achievements. Had fate not intervened, regarding his fight against cancer and brief spell away from The Den, his record, seemingly now unassailable, could have been far greater.

Listed are below are the clubs who provided the opposition, all 55 of them, and the 138 goals he scored against them in all competitions:

AFC Bournemouth	7	Macclesfield Town	2
AFC Wimbledon	1	Manchester City	1
Blackpool	2	Middlesbrough	1
Bradford City	3	Milton Keynes Dons	2
Brentford	5	Northampton Town	2
Brighton & Hove A	2	Norwich City	1
Bristol City	1	Nottingham Forest	3
Bristol Rovers	4	Notts County	2
Burnley	2	Oldham Athletic	6
Bury	5	Oxford United	4
Cambridge United	2	Reading	6
Cardiff City	5	Rotherham United	3
Carlisle United	3	Scunthorpe United	3
Chester City	1	Sheffield United	1
Colchester United	3	Stockport County	3
Coventry City	2	Stoke City	4
Crewe Alexandra	2	Swansea City	2
Crystal Palace	2	Swindon Town	1
Derby County	3	Tranmere Rovers	1
Exeter City	1	Walsall	5
Gillingham	4	Watford	1
Grimsby Town	2	West Ham United	1
Hartlepool United	4	Wigan Athletic	1
Huddersfield Town	1	Wimbledon	1
Ipswich Town	2	Wrexham	2
Leeds United	4	Wycombe Wanderers	3
Leigh RMI	1	York City	1
Luton Town	1		

BIBLIOGRAPHY

Batty, Clive, *The Chelsea Miscellany*, Vision Sports
    Publishing, 2006
Bolam, Mike, *The Newcastle Miscellany*, Vision Sports Publishing, 2007
Cameron Colin, *The Valiant 500*, self published, 1991
Collett, Mike, *The Complete Record of The FA Cup*, Sports Books, 2003
Giller, Norman, *McFootball: The Scottish Heroes of the English Game*,
    Robson Books, 2003
McCartney, Iain, *Manchester United – The Forgotten Fixtures*, Breedon
    Books, 2009
Mitten Andy, *The Man Utd Miscellany*, Vision Sports
    Publishing, 2007
Powley, Adam & Cloake, Martin, *The Spurs Miscellany,*
    Vision Sports Publishing 2007
Sherwin, Phil, *The Port Vale Miscellany*, The History Press, 2010
Tibballs, Geoff, *Football's Greatest Characters,* JR Books, 2008
Woodhall, Dave, *The Aston Villa Miscellany*, Vision Sports Publishing,
    2007
Millwall Football Club programmes - various issues